THE PRINCIPAL'S LEADERSHIP SOURCEBOOK

Practices, Tools, and Strategies for Building a Thriving School Community

EVAN ROBB

Foreword by Jim Burke

SCHOLASTIC

New York • Toronto • London • Auckland • Sydney
Mexico City • New Delhi • Hong Kong • Buenos Aires

Dedication

For my mother, with love and thanks for

believing I had a message to share.

For my wife, Cookie, for all her support and faith in me.

For Eleanor Smalley, superintendent of Clarke County Schools,

for allowing me to lead.

Editor: Sarah Glasscock
Cover design by Jason Robinson
Interior design by Teresa B. Southwell
Interior photographs by Bonnie Jacobs, copyright © 2007 by Bonnie Jacobs
ISBN-13: 978-0-439-70483-0
ISBN-10: 0-439-70483-9
Copyright © 2007 by Evan Robb

Table of Contents

Acknowledgments

The journey I have taken—a journey that started with substitute teaching and then moved to full-time positions as a history and language arts teacher—has shaped the values and beliefs I live by as a principal.

Many teachers and administrators have supported my journey and provided models of excellence that have influenced my leadership style. To Mary Ann Biggs, principal of Johnson Williams Middle School, in Berryville, Virginia, in the early 1990s, my thanks for providing the model of a compassionate principal who was always outside her office working with teachers and talking to students. It's Mary Ann who hired me for my first full-time teaching position and started me on this incredible journey, which has brought me full circle to Johnson Williams Middle School as its present principal.

My sincere thanks to Bill Flora, who was assistant superintendent in Warren County, Virginia, for encouraging me to apply for the position of assistant principal at the middle school, and to Andrew Keller, who worked side by side with me to open and staff Warren County Junior High School. Our friendship and candid relationship has enabled Andrew, now principal of Warren County Junior High, and me to support one another even though we lead different schools.

My deepest thanks go to Eleanor Smalley, superintendent of Clarke County Public Schools, who saw in me the leadership qualities that I didn't see in myself at that time. Thanks, too, for her good counsel, her faith in my leadership qualities, and her support and inspiration over the years we've worked together.

I must also thank the teachers and students I've worked with, for they have given me the knowledge necessary to lead effectively and compassionately.

And finally, to my wife, Cookie, my thanks for the patience and support she gave me while I was writing and revising this book.

— **Evan Robb**

Foreword

by Jim Burke

My first principal, Nancy Spaeth, set the standard for all who would follow. The year she hired me as a new teacher, she was elected Principal of the Year by her colleagues in California. In the 20 years since she hired me I have seen and worked with an array of principals, each of whom would have been a better principal for having read the book you hold in your hands. Evan Robb offers here what we all need in whatever domain we work: an essential guide, an almanac of wisdom, collected from his experience with underperforming schools (which, under his leadership, became thriving learning communities) and high-achieving schools.

A principal in the twenty-first century must do so much, be so many things: leader, role model, mentor, coach, disciplinarian, teacher, public relations wiz, data analyst, and politician. Evan Robb's description of what happens in the first *ten minutes* of a typical day leaves the reader exhausted--until you realize that what follows is a guide to help you master all those roles, even while answering the 50 e-mails waiting for you upon your arrival in the morning and preparing to address the concerns of the three mothers who were also awaiting your arrival. At the heart of this intelligent guide are the core principles Evan Robb outlines early on and then applies throughout the rest of the book.

It might strike you as curious that a teacher would be asked to write the foreword for a book about being an effective principal. First, I go to work every day at a school where I must rely on my principal to create and maintain a learning environment suitable to the academic demands schools now face. As a teacher I need the kind of principal Evan's book prepares one to be: responsive, intelligent, visionary but practical, supportive, and trustworthy. In addition to being a classroom teacher, I am also an author who spends time with teachers and administrators all over the country. When I come to work with a school I can tell within minutes if they have the culture and infrastructure to create the change they seek, for it is within the first few minutes that I meet and talk to the principal. Today's principal must be an instructional leader, one with a substantial knowledge of teaching and the disciplines as well as students and their learning needs. This book shows a new or evolving principal how to be that kind of leader by providing strategies and steps you can follow.

In addition to working with other schools, I have had the honor of participating on the hiring committee for principals at our school. This book reads like a recipe for the kind of principal we were asked to hire. In fact, the man we did hire would have found such a book as this invaluable. While he had distinguished himself as a teacher and assistant administrator, he was 31 and would be a first-time principal. I don't say he needed this book because he didn't know what to do. On the contrary, he has been a remarkable leader these last three years. But this book would have given him the resource that any principal would want upon arriving at a new school. Here is a wealth of practical strategies and checklists any principal can use for setting up committees or running effective meetings, evaluating teachers or managing school data to close the achievement gap.

This book does more than just offer useful checklists and tips of the trade. Evan Robb has profound insights into the psychology of the position. Every chapter examines the inherent complexity of the relationship between the principal and the people he or she must lead. He illustrates the political complexities of working with parents or teachers, using his "big six" principles that form the "core of effective leadership." Like Steven Covey, Evan consistently distinguishes between merely managing and actively leading according to these core principles. A principal who merely manages will tend to focus on scores and dollars, whereas a leader such as Evan describes will concentrate on the teachers and students, investing in that relationship with the knowledge that it will yield the results that others outside the school community expect.

Evan provides compelling examples of such relationships throughout the book. Focusing on the principal's relationship to his faculty, he recalls one instance in which a faculty member was going to be out for some time to care for his wife, who had been diagnosed with cancer. Evan called the faculty together and showed his commitment to them—and the individual teacher—by donating all his available sick days to a catastrophic sick leave bank and inviting others to contribute what they too could afford from their own. A principal's commitment to the students is, of course, no less crucial to a school's success. Every page of this book illustrates Evan's belief that each student in a school can succeed in the demanding academic environment common to all schools these days.

Every principal comes into the job wanting to make a difference, to lead the school and its surrounding community to a different, better place. Too often the principal, whether new or experienced, faces a world of demands and decisions, all of them important, all consequential, which can undermine or at least distract them from their greater vision of what the school could be. As I read this book, I thought over and over that this is the principal I would want to work for as a teacher, the one I would want to work with as a professional developer, and, perhaps most important, the one whose school I would want to send my three children to, for I would be confident that they would learn not just about reading and writing, arithmetic and history, but about themselves, the world, and their place within it. Isn't that what we all want, as teachers and parents, as citizens and politicians?

Time to go to the principal's office. . .but don't worry: Principal Robb is in and through this wonderful book, he'll be there whenever you need him.

Introduction

Whether you're an aspiring, new, or veteran principal, leadership is a word you will continually hear from the central office, other administrators, teachers, and parents. In fact, men and women receive promotions when their leadership is strong and lose jobs when it is lacking.

Leadership is a complex concept. Many books have been written on it, and most people agree that it is a key ingredient of success in any field. The question I would like you to consider is this: What are the core elements of outstanding school leadership? This book focuses on six core elements that are important to the success of school principals and administrators; in fact, they apply to any field. These elements should permeate your leadership style because each element defines who you are and what you believe in. These beliefs enable you to reach out to students, teachers, staff, parents, and your community. I believe that these core elements reside within most of us; sometimes we need to dig deeper to find and reclaim them.

The Big Six: The Core of Effective Leadership

1. Caring: It is crucial to care about and for others and to place their needs above our own. If a teacher's child or parent becomes ill, you can show you care by sending that teacher home and taking her classes.

2. Empathy: A close cousin of caring, empathy allows you to step into another person's shoes and understand issues from his perspective. Seeing your staff's issues through their eyes can enable you to find ways to give a stressed or sick person some paid time off or to make sure a child from a family where one breadwinner is out of work has boots and a winter coat.

3. Communication: The ability to communicate your message and concerns in a kind and considerate way can inspire members of your school community to do the same, and as a result, you will gain their respect. Be caring and empathetic when you have to deliver tough messages about such things as being on time in the morning or attending to recess duties. Speak to teachers privately and kindly and negotiate ways you can support positive change. In addition, always write a note or e-mail to acknowledge a job well done, a terrific display of students' work, or comments from parents and students about a particular teacher.

4. Passion: Be passionate about your job, and share your enthusiasm. Remember that passion and enthusiasm are infectious. You can communicate your passion for learning and making your school the best it can be during faculty meetings and administrative and parent meetings and by building consensus and making shared decisions.

5. Trust: Without trust, you cannot lead. Trust takes time to build and can be destroyed easily. Carry a pad and pencil with you when you walk around school. Jot down promises you make or teachers' request so you can ensure that you follow through.

6. Vision: Continually work with your staff and community to develop a shared vision that will rally everyone around ways to improve student achievement, teachers' instruction and professional growth, and community relations.

Note how the big six connect to one another. To quote an old song about love and marriage: "You can't have one without the other." The one word for me that tightly binds these six elements together is the word *all*. As principals, you and I want to provide learning opportunities and support for all students, all teachers, and all parents. This is a tall order, and it can be daunting at times.

I always strive for total congruence between what I say and what I do. For example, if I tell teachers that ongoing professional study can improve best practice, then I must make time during the contracted day to offer teachers the time and resources to study and to make each professional day an experience that inspires and develops their desire to improve. Give yourself the gift of time and understand that cultivating the big six is a continual obligation and goal.

When I first planned this book, I envisioned covering every aspect of the principal's job. That would have resulted in a huge book that collected dust on a shelf. With the help of my editor, Wendy Murray, I soon recognized that by covering less and being selective, I would produce a readable book that would support principals.

Throughout this book, I invite you into my school so you can learn about my leadership style. Each of the six chapters in this book contains stories, examples, and suggestions that have worked for me. I hope that they will affirm your strengths, as well as offer ideas that you can adapt to your own situation.

Equally important to note is that I have made mistakes along the way, but I've tried to rectify them and move forward. I hope, too, that this book will help you to avoid some pitfalls and achieve success for yourself, your students, your staff, and your community.

Chapter 1

Fifteen Must-Do Items for School Principals:

A July to Mid-September Agenda
That Leads to a Smooth School Year

• • •

There are no secrets to success. It is the result of preparation, hard work, and learning from failure.

- Colin Powell

I t's a crisp, fall day, and I'm on my way to work. My commute is short, so I try to use this time to review the upcoming day. Suddenly, my cell phone rings. My secretary, JoAnn, says that three angry parents are in the front office; each one is demanding to meet with me immediately. I reply that I'll be there shortly and will meet with them as soon as I can.

After arriving at school, I see Jesse Turner, one of my assistant principals. "Hey, what's going on?" he asks, smiling as he walks toward me.

"This is already shaping up to be a tough day," I tell Jesse. "I've got three upset parents waiting for me. Do you know anything about it?"

"Yep," Jesse says. "One parent feels his daughter was unfairly singled out in basketball practice. I think the guy just hates our new coach. He wanted to be the basketball coach. He even interviewed with the athletic department, but he didn't get the position because we always look for a teacher to coach instead of a parent."

I nod. "I'm not surprised about that one. What about the other two parents?"

"I had a meeting yesterday afternoon, and an issue with a substitute teacher surfaced," Jesse reveals. "She lost her temper and cursed at the class."

"Did you speak to her?" I ask.

"Yes, she felt bad. But I already called the personnel office to remove her from the list," Jesse replies.

"Good," I say. "What about the third parent?"

Jesse smiles. "Sorry, I don't know anything about that one."

As I enter the building, our custodian waves me into the bathroom to point out graffiti on the walls. I feel like he thinks I can snap my fingers to catch who did it. Of course, finding the culprit isn't that simple. I ask the custodian to wipe off the graffiti and let me know if it happens again. Proceeding to my office, I make a mental note that our hall duty teacher isn't present. Three teachers stroll by me. I nod and wish them a good morning but don't stop. As I continue to walk to my office, bent on meeting quickly with the three parents, I hope my teachers understand my haste.

I turn the corner leading to my office, and a teacher stops me. "Mr. Robb, why did you allow that parent to just come in and sit in my room yesterday?" she asks. Her voice is shaky and nervous.

"I have no idea what you're talking about, but I'll catch up with you later this morning," I assure her. "I've got three parents in my office who are waiting to see me."

I open the office door. Sure enough, three unhappy parents are sitting on chairs. JoAnn motions me toward her. "Evan, we had two teachers call in sick this morning. It's too late to get subs for them now. Also, there aren't any lesson plans on file for them."

"Didn't we send a memo requesting that all teachers turn in emergency lesson plans to my assistant?" I ask.

"I sent the memo, but only half the teachers turned them in."

That's just great, I think. I'm beginning to feel totally frustrated.

"You also have messages. The last five came in while you were at that meeting yesterday," JoAnn says as she hands them to me.

I greet each parent and shake hands. Then I explain that because the buses are unloading, I need to be in the hallways to monitor behavior and to support my teachers. "I can see you in fifteen minutes," I tell them. "If that's a problem, I'll do my best to accommodate your needs." All three say they can wait, and I'm relieved that only two weeks into the school year, I will be able to supervise the start of the day.

Just then my secretary announces, "Mr. Robb, you have a phone call. It's the superintendent."

"I'll take it in my office," I tell her, knowing that a call from the superintendent this early in the morning must be important.

"Good morning, Evan. How are things going?" the superintendent asks.

"Just great," I say, not wanting to communicate my stress to him.

"Evan, I need you to present at our school board meeting tonight. I want you to review and update your school improvement plan. Remember, it starts at seven p.m.; make sure you're there by six thirty."

"Fine, I'll see you tonight." I remember that I was planning on taking my wife to dinner. I'll have to give her a call to cancel.

I turn on my walkie-talkie and hear my assistant's voice say, "We just had a fight."

"Where did it occur?" I ask.

"By the front hallway," Jesse answers. "Why isn't the duty teacher here?"

"I have no idea. Can you handle this one? I'll get there when I can. I've still got those parents in my office," I remind him.

By this time, I've given up on hall duty. Before I call my secretary to send in the first parent, I check my e-mail. I can't believe it: I've got 50 e-mails! They'll have to wait. I call my secretary. "Ask the parent who arrived first to come to my office."

The events of that morning can happen in elementary, middle, or high school. The athletic issue would probably not crop up in elementary school, but another one could be substituted easily, such as parents' insisting their child be in the top reading group. It's important to view these events in a realistic time frame. What occurred from the time I walked into the school to the point I asked that the first parent be ushered into my office took about ten minutes. Including the presentation to the school board, my school day didn't end until after nine that evening.

The principal's job will challenge you, both physically and mentally. It's a job that starts on July 1 (unless you're in a year-round school) and requires communication and decision-making skills that you'll acquire from on-the-job experience. No graduate class can replace experience. Although no two years are alike, your primary goal each year should be to make decisions that are in the best interest of your students. Such decision-making starts in the summer, before students and staff enter the building, and continues throughout the year. Taking the time to build positive relationships with all the members of your school and the surrounding community *before school opens* becomes the firm foundation that enables you to lead effectively. You will have cultivated the support and understanding of your staff and parents, and they will support you throughout the year.

Fifteen Items to Complete Between July 1 and Mid-September

By mid-September, I try to have these 15 items in place. I keep a list of them, and as each initiative is begun, I check it off. Revisiting the list twice a month allows me to make sure that I'm following up with various groups to ask for feedback, to monitor their progress with a project, and to write thank-you e-mails. Thanking people in writing shows that you value their contributions to school life and honors the extra work and commitment they've made to support teachers and students.

1: Forge bonds with staff who work during the summer.

When you are the new principal, people will make judgments about you based on first impressions and their perceptions of why you were hired. As a principal, it's important to learn to accept the fact that you have little control over the assumptions that people make about you. You do have complete control over how you present yourself to your staff day in and day out.

A new principal should begin to get to know her staff immediately. Since most teaching staff is not at school in July, this is the ideal time to get to know other staff members who are equally important: secretaries, additional office staff who may be present for part of the summer, custodians, guidance counselors, and your assistant principals. Building relationships takes time and should not be forced; open communication and a friendly demeanor help the process.

If you don't know your assistant principals, begin to interact with them quickly. I like to eat lunch with them off campus on the first day. Leaving school is a good way to get know each other and to find out about their job responsibilities. First, there are no telephone calls or other interruptions so your lunch can proceed smoothly. Second, meeting and dining off campus is more relaxing, and conversations tend to be candid because you have privacy.

Keep in mind that an assistant principal may have applied for the principal's position, or he may have been on the interview committee and wanted another candidate. Do not put time into finding out if that is the case. Focus on connecting, clarifying job responsibilities, and communicating your style and hopes. If assistants have worked in the school before, find out what their key job responsibilities were. Did they enjoy them? Do they want more challenges? If so, what kinds of challenges do they seek?

Over time, working together with your staff will build a positive and meaningful relationship. One way for you to foster this is by being yourself.

2: Take extra time to form solid relationships with secretaries.

I suggest meeting individually with secretaries on July 1 or your first day on the job. At this first meeting, I usually tell stories about my family and myself. Sometimes this personal sharing is reciprocated, but sometimes it's not; accept the level of sharing your secretaries offer.

The following questions can help you involve your secretary in decisions about her position:

- What have been your main responsibilities?
- Are there any new responsibilities that you'd like?
- What would you like to see done differently this year?

● Has meeting the needs of students, staff, and parents been the primary focus at the school? If so, how has this been accomplished?

These questions can give a new principal a great deal of information. Since it's important that this meeting not feel like a job interview to your secretary, begin with only one or two questions.

3: Circulate and meet staff in the first two weeks of July.

Even if your office is piled high with boxes and you feel compelled to rummage through them to organize files or read e-mail, set aside these urges and make yourself visible and available to everyone at school during the first two weeks of July. By making the rounds and chatting with staff, you send the powerful message that they are far more important to you than administrative detail work. This means that you might have to remain at school after staff leaves to organize your office. Do it.

The three suggestions below have helped me during the first two weeks of the new school year.

Be friendly, upbeat, and positive with everyone you meet. On your first day, several staff members will come by to meet you shortly after you arrive. Make time to say hello and chat with each one. If you appear to be too busy, your staff may assume that you won't be available the rest of the year either. When you converse with staff, keep the conversation light—inquire about their summer and their families.

Avoid answering school-related questions during the first few days, for you don't want to give a misinformed answer. Say something like *That's a great topic for our first faculty meeting* or *Let's bring that up when your department meets* or *I'll need more time to think about that suggestion*. Note and date every suggestion so you can follow up on it. Saying you'll follow up and not doing so can start negative talk among your staff.

Remember that staff members have their own agendas for a first-day visit to the new or experienced principal. As principal you have no control over that; however, you do have control over presenting an interested and upbeat impression.

Do your best to remember names. All staff members will know you and expect you to know them. This is a challenge; do your best. Walk around and speak with people. I find that chatting and gathering stories about people helps me remember their names. People in the school will want to meet the new principal and see what you're about. New staff and parents new to the community will want to meet you, too. Remember, when a new principal comes to the job, people may feel happy, sad, nervous, or anxious—especially if they've respected and loved the former principal. Their first impressions of you will either confirm or remove their anxiety.

Make sure that you dress appropriately. During July and August, your clothing should not be a suit or a blazer and tie. I dress casually during my first days on the job as I'm usually carrying boxes from my car to my office or rearranging things in my office after everyone leaves.

4: Use a checklist to evaluate your readiness.

By the middle of July, I review a checklist like the one shown below to make sure that I've addressed each statement. This list becomes my memory, which is far safer than rummaging through my mind to recall details. It also ensures that I won't forget a key point.

Statements	Status	
1. I have a filing system in place.	Yes	No
2. My computer is set up with a log-in.	Yes	No
3. I have moved necessary personal items into my office.	Yes	No
4. I am familiar with the school's layout.	Yes	No
5. I have inspected all classrooms.	Yes	No
6. The school is fully staffed.	Yes	No
7. The central office has all my paperwork.	Yes	No
8. I am presenting myself professionally and with confidence.	Yes	No
9. I am getting to know staff and parents.	Yes	No
10. I am starting to plan ahead.	Yes	No
11. I have a calendar system in place.	Yes	No
12. I have reviewed files that were left in my office.	Yes	No
13. I have had casual discussions with my assistant.	Yes	No
14. I have met with office staff.	Yes	No

It's difficult to have all of these items marked yes by mid-July, but the list can guide you in prioritizing. During July, you're meeting staff and parents. In addition, several staff members are working with you on summer initiatives. Remember that everyone you work with draws conclusions about you and communicates their perceptions to other staff. This is the ideal time to be a good listener and a hard worker and to show empathy when teachers and parents raise issues and concerns.

5: Compose and mail welcome letters to parents and staff.

When parents receive a letter from you inviting them to drop by and spend time with you, it sends the message that you are available and looking forward to meeting and working with them. Be wary, however, of committing to something in the letter that you cannot accomplish.

Dear Parents,

I am excited to be starting my new job as school principal. My first week on the job has been a busy one. I have met many students, staff members, and parents. All of this leads me to believe that I will thoroughly enjoy my new position. I will have a newsletter out shortly to let you know key dates, such as the following: registration, our Back to School Night, and athletic tryouts.

Please feel free to come by the school to meet with me. I will do my best to answer any questions that you might have.

Sincerely,
Evan Robb
School Principal

The Principal's Leadership Sourcebook

Sending a letter to your staff is equally important. Some staff will have met you during your first two weeks; others may not have the opportunity to come to the school until opening meetings. A welcome letter gives everyone the chance to meet you.

Dear Staff,

I hope that you have been enjoying your summer break. I'm sure all of us are amazed at how quickly the summer is going by. Soon we'll be back in school, beginning what I am sure will be an excellent year. Many of you have visited me already, and I appreciate how welcoming you've been. Often, when new leadership comes to a school, it can be a time of anxiety and nervousness. This goes both ways. I can assure you that I'll do my best to make the transition a smooth one for all of us.

I look forward to working with all of you to make an already excellent school even better! There are only two types of schools in America: those that are improving and those that are declining. There is no middle ground. Given that choice, our path is an obvious one—to improve our school by working together. Improvement is a never-ending journey. Focusing on improvement assures us that each year we move closer to our common goals.

Kind regards,
Evan Robb
School Principal

Both letters can and should be adjusted to meet your needs. I suggest mailing the parent letter and the staff letter by the middle of July.

6: Meet your parents by organizing Meet the Principal sessions.

It's mid-July. You've met many staff members and sent letters to parents and staff. Now it's time to get to know more parents by organizing informal Meet the Principal sessions. These get-togethers are opportunities for parents to meet you and for you to answer some questions that might be on their minds. I recommend setting up two sessions at the end of July. Set one meeting in the morning and another meeting in the late afternoon. Staggering times increases the chances of more parents coming. Meet the Principal gatherings are a great way to start your first principal's position or to connect with new and returning parents if you are a veteran principal.

I recommend that you practice your presentation, especially if this is your first time talking before parents. Feeling comfortable in this type of meeting takes time, but I've come to enjoy the opportunity to meet with parents. I've also found these meetings helpful for enlisting parents to volunteer in the school. After these sessions, I've always received positive feedback from parents because they've made a personal connection with me, and I with them.

As part of your presentation, make sure to give those in attendance the date of the next meeting and to encourage parents to bring a friend to the next meeting. When your presentation is over, mingle with parents but try not to let one or two people monopolize your time. These events work best when the principal circulates among as many parents as possible.

Some questions that new administrators frequently ask me about organizing these Meet the Principal gatherings and my responses appear below.

How do I get the word out about these sessions?

If your school publishes a newsletter, announce the meetings in its pages accompanied by an introduction to you. If you have a school Web site or access to a local television channel, use these, too. Post a start time and a finish time for the meeting; one hour usually works well. Let parents know that the meeting is informal.

Should I have refreshments?

Yes, but keep them simple. Coffee is a good choice for both the morning and early afternoon. Serve donuts or bagels in the morning and cookies in the afternoon. School budget money can be used for refreshments. I use money that's part of our school bank account, not money that requires a purchase order. Procedures in your school system may vary so find the answer before you start to spend. If your parent organization is already up and running, parents will be happy to assist.

What do I talk about?

Talk about yourself: Include your educational background and some information about your family. Assure people that you're excited and want to work with them for the success of the school and their children. Encourage them to get involved either as a volunteer in classes or with a parent-advisory group. If you have a parent organization leader, invite her to make a brief presentation. Remember to meet her before this meeting and mutually agree on guidelines and time limits for the talk. Have sign-up forms available for parent volunteers to complete. (See Appendix A, p. 163).

FREQUENTLY ASKED QUESTIONS AT MEET THE PRINCIPAL GATHERINGS

Most parent questions at these meetings are general and can be addressed with a short response. Here are some frequently asked questions that can help you better prepare for these meetings.

- Do you have an open-door policy?
- How can I get involved as a volunteer?
- Can I take my child for a walk through the school before it opens?
- How will the school keep me informed?

Unexpected questions can also surface. If you don't know an answer, that's fine. Take the parent's phone number and say that you will call with the answer the next day. As the new principal, no one expects you to have an answer for everything.

7. Continue connecting by starting a parent-advisory group.

Many partnerships are necessary for a successful school: community partnerships, business partnerships, and a strong partnership with parents. The parent partnership is critical, and parents need to perform meaningful tasks in the school. What I am looking for are true partnerships, where all players—students, teachers, administrators, and parents—have the same goal of a quality education for all children. The more parents are involved and understand how the school works, operates, and communicates, the better the chances for an effective partnership with them.

One of the best ways to accomplish this is with a parent-advisory group. This group will support and advise you on fund-raising and communication. They also will provide refreshments for faculty meetings and special school events such as Back to School Night. Whether your group is new or established, meeting with them should be a priority in July.

Parent support is vital to your position, but note that participation by parents tends to decrease as students progress through school. You can reverse this trend and form a well-organized parent group that works for the benefit of your school community by considering the suggestions in Tip 8.

8: Make the parent advisory group productive.

● ● ●

These guidelines for working with a parent advisory group have worked well for me. As you'll see, communication and following up on requests and decisions are key.

- Get to know the members of the group. Make sure you communicate your enthusiasm for their work and that you look forward to being involved with the group.
- Find out the meeting schedule for the group, and mark the dates on your calendar. Build the schedule into your calendar for the year, and try to attend every meeting.
- Ask the parents how the previous principal worked with them and what their expectations are for working with you. Openly and positively share your thoughts on how you would like to work with their group. Always build consensus between parents and you through discussion and by truly using them in an advisory capacity.
- Find out how the group communicates with other parents. Do they use the school Web site or a newsletter? What has worked in the past? What are their suggestions for improving communication?
- Discover parents' goals and what changes need to be made to achieve them.
- Explain your Meet the Principal sessions, and encourage members to attend and to spread the word about the advisory group.

9: Structure the parent advisory group.

● ● ●

I find that ten members is an ideal number for an effective advisory group. All advisory groups should appoint officers, meet on a regular basis, and start recruiting more parents.

If the number increases or you have a large number of interested parents immediately, then you'll need to organize subcommittees. I prefer to organize one executive committee that meets once a month as well as several subcommittees, each of which is headed by a member of the executive committee. Subcommittees can meet less often and will appeal to those parents who can't commit to an established meeting schedule. Each year, I set up the following subcommittees:

Academic Committee: I brief this subcommittee on the academic programs and academic progress of the school, including data from testing. Often, I invite teachers to attend these meetings to share exciting things going on in their classes and to field some questions from parents. This group also can be used to review textbooks for adoption and to offer advice on the academic direction of the school. It should meet after school, as teachers find it difficult to attend later meeting times.

Hospitality Committee: This subcommittee is made up of parents who assist with teacher recognition and support school events such as coordinating refreshments for special ceremonies, preparing faculty dinners on conference nights, and planning Teacher Appreciation Week.

Fund-Raiser Committee: I challenge this group to coordinate at least two school fund-raisers for the year. These might include organizing a school dance or a more traditional fund-raiser that involves the selling of goods. To see what teachers need each year, I send out a staff e-mail in early September and ask teachers to create a wish list of items that would benefit their teaching. Then I give this list to the chair of the committee. The chair shares this list with committee members, and they prioritize the distribution of money.

10: If there is no parent advisory group, establish one.

This can happen if your school is new or if a previous principal chose not to have a parent advisory group. In this case, set a goal for starting a group during the second half of July. You can use the following suggestions as guidelines:

- Consult a central office colleague, the previous principal, or a current staff member to find out the names of several parents who might be interested in getting involved. Call them, introduce yourself, and ask if they'd like to meet with you to discuss starting a parent advisory group. Explain that this is a way to support and to advise you on issues such as how the school communicates with parents, fund-raising, extracurricular activities, and textbook adoption.

- Encourage these parents to attend the Meet the Principal sessions. Give parents an overview of how the group can be structured at the session, and let them know that you value this partnership. Have a sign-up sheet available for parents to write their names, phone numbers, and e-mail addresses if they're interested.
- Set a date for your first meeting: it should fall about a week after your second Meet the Principal session and within a week of your initial phone call.
- Your first meeting should be brief. Let parents know how you'd like to structure the advisory group, either as one group or as an executive group and subcommittees. Encourage volunteers to speak to other parents if you need to enlarge membership.

I've always had success with this method of starting a parent group. Parents who attend the Meet the Principal sessions are usually willing to participate in a parent-advisory group. After the second Meet the Principal session, send an upbeat, follow-up e-mail to all the parents who signed up. Thank them for their interest, and remind them of the date and time of their first parent advisory group meeting.

11: Manage your school budget.

Getting a handle on your school budget can be complex. In most schools, money comes from two sources: the school board and fees and other fund-raising activities. Spending money wisely takes good planning. If there aren't any procedures for accessing and handling money, problems can develop. School money that's handled well should assist the needs of teachers and students. There is never a limitless amount of money; watchful management ensures that you'll have enough dollars to meet teachers' and students' needs all year long.

I'll refer to money from the school board as operational money. To access this money, you must complete a purchase order. Money generated from book fees, fund-raisers, school pictures, and so on, is money that most schools keep in a local bank. Usually, the principal has check-writing privileges for these funds. Make sure that you understand your district's method of organizing its schools' budgets. Doing this will enable you to maintain accurate records that follow district procedures.

During the summer, you'll want to make sure you've addressed the following items. Doing so will familiarize you with your school district's financial systems and enable you to run a financially secure school.

- Review your operational budget and seek out another principal or central office employee who can meet with you to explain any questions.
- Understand how that budget is categorized.
- Look at the most recent audit of school funds and identify issues that the audit has not addressed.
- Go to the bank to add your signature to the school's checking account if one exists. *It is important to require two signatures on a check. Most auditors recommend this.*
- Ask the bookkeeper to show you clear examples of procedures for placing purchase orders and reimbursement. (See Appendix B, p. 164, for examples of procedures you can use for handling your school money.)

12: Avoid these four common school finance pitfalls.

Saying yes to all requests you receive. Never mislead people into thinking that you can meet all requests, for there is a limit to how much money is available. If you find that you say yes too often, I recommend taking another look at your procedures for requests. This is a good opportunity to review procedures and to assure staff members that instead of receiving random requests, your goal is to set aside money for all the needs in your school. Your staff needs to follow these procedures; using them will assure that everyone has equal access to money.

Permitting purchase requests to circumvent the principal. Clear procedures should assure that the principal reviews all requests. In some schools, the bookkeeper makes the determinations for requests. I do not recommend this. The principal has a bottom-line responsibility to manage the budget; do not relinquish that role. Work with your bookkeeper to change this procedure. By explaining your responsibilities and offering to work with the bookkeeper as a team, you can create change without hurting your working relationship. Communicate the adjustments to staff when they return in August.

Failing to allow teams or departments to decide what they need. No school can be effective if the principal makes most of the decisions. Experience has shown me that my staff members are aware of their instructional needs—if effective school improvement has taken place over the summer. Good improvement plans can direct a department or team of teachers to the materials they require to meet the goals of the plan. (See Chapter 2 for information on school summer-improvement planning.)

An easy way to empower departments is to send a letter to each department (or grade-level leader) that allocates the amount of money it receives. At my school, the number of teachers in a department determines the amount of money it receives. My faculty and I feel that solution is fair because the more teachers, the more materials needed (See Appendix C, p. 165, for an example of a letter explaining to staff how I've allocated money.) However, if a department disagrees with its funding, my door is always open and teachers can state their needs to me. It's important to listen and to resolve perceptions of unfairness on your part. Because I do not release all of the funds at the start of the year, I have the flexibility to address these kinds of needs.

Spending too much money too quickly. Central offices fix the amount of money in a school's operational budget for the year. Effectively managing this money is critical. Spending too much at the start of the year can force the principal to be very tight with money later on. I suggest looking at the total amount of money in the operational budget and not exceeding 70 percent of that until early March. Many central offices will set a percentage for you to stay within, which protects a new or an experienced principal. If your central office does not set budget parameters, then I advise you to set them yourself. It's important to make your bookkeeper aware of these. And finally, requesting monthly expenditure reports from your bookkeeper or your district's finance department is an excellent way to assess how much money is available.

13: Make preparations for school fee week in August.

• • •

Many schools across our country charge student fees at registration. These fees cover consumable instructional costs, such as workbooks and science and art supplies. Fee week will bring many parents to the school, so it's a good time to advertise upcoming events, such as Back to School Night, and to have parent representatives present to encourage other parents to join a parent advisory subcommittee or to sign up as a volunteer.

The following suggestions can enable you to prepare adequately for a smooth fee week:

- Establish and communicate times when parents can pay school fees. One or two days of fee week should have hours later than 4:00 p.m. to accommodate working parents. Communicate these dates and times in a newsletter or school mailing, or through a group mailing if that's done by your central office.
- Hand out students' schedules during fee week. (It's important to coordinate this timeline with your guidance department.)
- Ask your parent advisory group to assist with collecting fees and handing out students' schedules.
- Put your bookkeeper in charge of counting and depositing the money into your school's bank account. If fee sheets need to be ordered, do this at least two weeks prior to fee week.

14: Plan Back to School Night.

• • •

The beginning of August is the ideal time to organize your Back to School Night. I prefer to hold this special evening for students and parents about one week before school starts. Planning will help make the evening successful. Back to School Night should achieve these simple goals. Attending parents will do the following:

- Meet their child's teachers by walking their child's schedule.
- Hear the principal speak briefly and have the opportunity to meet with her.
- Feel comfortable with the school, teachers, and what will happen on the first day of school.

Principals who have been in the same school for several years have a feel for how these nights should go. This annual event can be more challenging for a new principal. Most likely, unless the school is new, an established routine for how these evenings should run is already in place. Therefore, it's very important to find out the procedures for these nights.

Unless you've heard they were awful, I would keep the routine the same. In my most recent position, I found out that a team leader in my school had prepared a PowerPoint presentation in the previous year that could be adjusted for the new school year. I set up a meeting with the team leader to review how the evening had been organized. Keeping the structure honors past procedures and those who developed them.

Here are some tried-and-true guidelines that can help you orchestrate a successful Back to School Night.

- Establish a date and time, and advertise the event. In my current school, I publish the date in our summer newsletter, do an additional mailing a week before the event, and post the date in the school office. Scrolling such dates on a school Web site is an excellent idea, if you have that option.

- Make sure that your Back to School Night doesn't conflict with the date set by other schools in your district. If several schools have these events on the same night, it will cause difficulty for parents who have children in two or more schools. Good communication can help avoid this. Some larger districts set Back to School Nights through a central calendar.

- Confirm that your auditorium or designated space is available. School auditoriums get used a great deal in smaller communities. Make sure that you know whom to contact for setting up a microphone, lighting, and a PowerPoint projector and screen.

- Contact your parent organization president. Let him know the date and discuss the group's involvement. In the past, I usually have had group members do a presentation in order to encourage other parents to join the group. I encourage the organization's president to speak at an agreed-upon time during the evening. Since this event has a large turnout, it's a good time to get parents involved. I always offer to make the parent-advisory group pitch for the president if he isn't comfortable speaking in front of large crowds.

- Schedule a time to meet with people you are relying on before the events to make sure things are in order.

- Have a plan for how parents will move about the school. Make printed school maps available. On my first Back to School Night, I didn't have a solid plan, and parents were everywhere. Now I have parents follow their child's schedule; they switch from class to class every five to seven minutes. Decide on how you'll signal class changes: Does your school have tones or bells, or will you use the PA system?

- Require professional dress for yourself and the entire staff.
- Circulate, greet people, and generate enthusiasm about the evening.
- End on time; staff and parents will appreciate this. To bring the event to a close, make an announcement such as this: *Thank you for attending our Back to School Night. Attendance tonight means a great deal to me personally and to the staff of this school. It's (designated end time), so we need to bring our evening to a close. I look forward to your continued involvement with our school this year.*

Details are critical when planning a Back to School Night. Several years ago, I checked the auditorium the day before our Back to School Night at around seven p.m. and noticed that it felt hot. The next day I called maintenance and found out the air-conditioning was on a timer that was set through a computer on the other side of the school. Until then, I hadn't known that I needed to adjust the cooling system. If I hadn't noticed how hot it was in the auditorium, my first Back to School Night would have been a disaster. (See Appendix D, pp. 166–167 for suggestions for your speech to parents and what to include in a PowerPoint presentation.)

15: Meet every student in your school.

By mid-September, you should have interacted with every student in your school. For the principal of a large school, this can be a daunting goal. The first step I take to achieve this goal is to don a chef's hat and apron on the second day of school. For two weeks, I help serve breakfast and lunch to every student. I'm serving them repeatedly and having short chats with each one.

In addition, I recommend that you greet students in the morning and afternoons as they walk off or on school buses. There will be times when meetings or emergencies take you away from talking to students as they arrive and depart. Be there as often as you can, for frequent contacts build solid relationships. You should also visit classes daily and be highly visible during changes of classes. When you're out of your office and interacting with students and staff, you build trust and send everyone the message that both students and staff are important to you. Moreover, counseling a student in trouble or one who needs your advice and support becomes easier when bonds have been established.

If a teacher is sick, try to take all or some of his classes. That's another way to deepen your relationships with students and show faculty that you care about them. During my second year as principal of Warren County Junior High, a history teacher told me that his wife had pancreatic cancer and they didn't have the insurance to hire caretakers. At our next faculty meeting, I asked each staff member to contribute one or two sick day, and I contributed all of mine to set an example. The teacher lost no salary while caring for his wife. Another history teacher and I covered his classes until he returned. I viewed this as a great way to support my teacher and to develop more meaningful relationships with students.

I believe that showing, by your actions, that you care about every member of your community and that you are willing to work harder to support your staff and students, is the kind of leadership that generates commitment among the entire school community.

Continue to Think About . . .

This chapter reviews the key items that any principal needs to consider at the beginning of a new job or when gearing up throughout the summer. I cannot stress enough how important it is to use summer time effectively. Planning with purpose and high expectations should be your primary focus. As this chapter points out, successful use of summer time requires a conceptual idea of what needs to be done and an organized plan to move forward.

This is a good time to reflect on the following key questions:

● Am I pleased with how I have used my summer time? Have I made notes to myself on what went well and what I need to improve for next summer?

● How does my staff view me? Are they seeing me the way I want them to perceive me? (Remember, this is something that a principal always has control over.)

● Am I doing my best to set the stage for a successful school opening?

Chapter 2

Defining Your Goals and Creating a Mission Statement

• • •

Determine the specific goal you want to achieve.
Then dedicate yourself to its attainment with unswerving
singleness of purpose, the trenchant seal of a crusade.

- Paul J. Meyer

fter my first year as assistant principal of Warren County Middle School, the superintendent offered me the job of principal at Warren County Junior High School. At that point, the construction of the junior high school was at its midway point. I accepted because the prospect of choosing my staff and shaping the goals and vision of a new school with them was a journey I longed to take. Although the building, its furnishings, and staff all would be new, the achievement and motivation of the students we were to serve would not change.

During the summer that I assumed the position of principal, I reviewed the test scores of the incoming eighth and ninth graders. To classify these scores as poor was an understatement. Standardized test scores in some areas, such as algebra and history, were as low as 15 percent; other areas ranged from 15 percent to 50 percent. Let me give meaning to these percentages: Virginia is a state that requires a passing rate of 70 percent or better for each test given in a school. As you can see, many students were far below this basic benchmark.

Five years later, our school had no scores lower than 80 percent, and many scores were in the 90 percent range. And compared with other schools in our area, our staff turnover was low—below 5 percent.

How did the staff and I accomplish this change? Frankly, through hard work as a cohesive team that focused entirely on student learning. The student population had not changed. What had changed was the level of instruction, the use of data analysis of student assessments, and the development of a mission statement that bonded staff with the common belief that they could improve the achievement of all students. So the results of staff and administrative collaboration connected the teaching community to an agreed-upon mission that became the beacon for ongoing professional learning and a renewed instructional commitment to every student.

As I look back on that first summer, I believe that setting goals and focusing the school on a mission of achievement for all laid the foundation for the improvement that occurred.

When I came to my current school, I wondered if the approach of being mission-directed, along with setting clear goals, would achieve similar success. This school has a different population: it's more affluent and has a long-standing culture of high student achievement. The first year, we set ourselves on a path to make an already strong school into an exceptional one. Our results were superb. We finished the year with the highest standardized scores in our area. Now the challenge is to continue to do better each year. Time will tell, but as I reflect I am even more confident that setting goals and having a clear sense of mission are the key factors in assuring a school's future success.

In this chapter, I'll share many tips and suggestions that can help you draft your own personal goals. In addition, I'll offer proactive suggestions for working on your school mission statement. By proactive, I mean purposeful planning with members of the school and outside community.

These two key responsibilities will need your attention as the year begins.

1. **Set professional and personal goals for the year.** These are goals that you set for yourself. They include your responsibilities as principal and your responsibility to your family and your community.

2. **Develop an effective school mission statement.** Remember, a mission statement and personal goals give direction for the year and can be your compass for your first year and beyond.

Balancing Short-Term and Long-Term Responsibilities

Leadership Tip:
Getting Your School Ready for Opening Day

The building facilities must be cleaned for the first day of school. Often, this requires having custodians work on a weekend; however, some schools don't pay overtime. If overtime isn't an option, then I recommend meeting with the custodial staff to reorganize their duties so the offices, hallways, cafeteria, and classrooms are ready for parents and students.

The principal's position can be overwhelming at times. At the beginning of the school year, it's easy to get caught up with short-term items that need a quick fix. I don't intend to imply that short-term responsibilities such as returning phone calls or addressing the myriad questions that come your way every day are unimportant. What I want you to consider is balancing short-term demands that often require quick decisions with long-term demands that require a slower and more thoughtful process. For example, the goal of adjusting or creating a mission statement is a long-term responsibility: it requires planning with a purpose. If you don't set out to accomplish these long-term goals, time will slip away and they may never be achieved.

The box below lists some short- and long-term goals. This is not a comprehensive list; view it as a beginning. As you review the goals, you'll notice that each item is important in order for a school to be able to operate. (It's easy to see how the short-term responsibilities can swallow up all your time.)

Short-Term Responsibilities

- Are we fully staffed?

- If the office staff is new, does everyone know my expectations?

- Have I met with new staff? Do we have a mentor program?

- Have I clarified the roles of administrators?

- Have I taken care of duty assignments?

- Are all our coaching positions filled?

- Do teachers know which rooms they are in?

- Have teachers been briefed on the procedures for the first days of school?

- Are schedules ready to print?

- Do we have a procedure for giving out class schedules to parents and students?

- Is the building clean?

- Are our heating and cooling systems working properly?

- Have we ordered all the consumable items we need?

- Are our computers ready for use?

- Do we have enough textbooks?

- Is our school Web site up-to-date? Who updates it?

Long-Term Responsibilities

- Have we looked at last year's data to adjust the instructional plan?

- Do I know our academic areas of strengths and weaknesses?

- How will we address students who are having challenges?

- Do I have a professional development plan for the school?

- Have departments and teams formulated goals for the year?

- Is our curriculum aligned and paced for the year ahead?

- Have we discussed expectations for student discipline?

- Does the staff understand the evaluation process?

- Do we have structures in place for meeting schedules?

- How are teachers communicating the curriculum to students and parents?

- Do we all have a sense of our purpose/mission as a school?

- Have I worked on ways to involve parents?

I reread the list weekly to ensure that I'm adding key items and addressing long-term responsibilities. Addressing the long-term items can create positive change such as the rising test scores we experienced at my junior high school. However, I don't intend to diminish the importance of finding a balance between short- and long-term considerations. For instance, at my current school, I'm in charge of monitoring all financial accounts, which includes postage. As the time for mailing report cards arrives, it's my job to make sure there's enough money to cover the cost. Minor items such as this one can gain importance at different points in the year. Revisiting your lists weekly will enable you to monitor these items and to keep abreast of the important parts of your day-to-day job.

Dealing With Unexpected Central Office Requests

• • •

Sometimes forces outside of school nudge you to move forward with goals and a mission statement before you've had time to consider them. I've experienced this and can recall the moment vividly.

It was the middle of August, and my day at Warren County Junior High had started quietly. After lunch, I received a telephone call from the assistant superintendent requesting me to put together my goals for my first year as principal. The next day, I was to meet with the superintendent to present them. Later that week, along with the other principals, I was to explain my goals to the school board. My frustration and anxiety level escalated when, minutes later, several teachers stopped by my office and asked, "Do we have a mission statement that we can hang in our class?"

Thoughts pummeled my brain—thoughts I knew I had to keep to myself. This was a new school, and we didn't have a mission statement formulated yet. At that point, the staff did not have to be in school, so how could I gather them to help create goals and discuss a mission statement? Moreover, I didn't know my teachers well. Would any of them come in early? Should I create a mission for them or try to buy myself some time? Thinking about personal goals was even more challenging. What did my superintendent want to see? I had no guide to use for a format. Both were hard questions to answer, especially when there was no time for building consensus to frame a mission statement and even less time to consider my personal goals. I envisioned my first formal meeting with the superintendent as being one big flop.

Over time, I've learned that it's okay to say, *I don't have that now* or *I need time to create my goals.* But in my first year as a principal, I felt that I had no choice but to comply with the request of the central office and my staff. It's important to mention here that some central offices will not give you additional time; sometimes a new principal just has to get things moving. It often seems to me that there's more understanding in our profession of the needs of new teachers but a limited understanding of what new principals need to grow into their jobs. Because a principal's salary is larger, there's an expectation that he can do it all. I felt the pressure of that expectation and didn't ask for extra time to form personal goals, nor did I build consensus among staff for creating a mission statement.

To put it simply, my goal was just to keep my head above water. (That was one goal I wouldn't share with my superintendent!) As I look back, I handled both requests poorly. To create a mission statement, a small committee did an Internet search, studied mission statements from other schools, drafted one for our school, and presented the results to staff members. This satisfied the central office, but in terms of using it to guide our first year, the mission statement was completely worthless. My personal goals were another matter. I didn't have a sense of the big picture for my first school year or beyond. I struggled in framing my goals, and they too were poor.

In my current position, a similar situation happened. I started my job on July 1. Within a week, a central office staff member called me and said, "We'll be having our administrative retreat shortly, and all principals will present their goals for the year." Fortunately, I had five years' experience in dealing with that request on short notice and was able to frame goals within three days. Moreover, as soon as I accepted my new position, I had begun drafting goals because I knew they would have to be completed prior to the opening of school. Most likely, you'll receive one of these phone calls: be prepared mentally to deal with it.

Goals for the Principal: A Pathway to Success

On the wall opposite my desk, I've posted the following quote by William Faulkner:

I have found that the greatest help in meeting any problem with decency and self-respect and what ever courage is demanded, is to know where you yourself stand. That is, to have in words what you believe and are acting from.

Clearly knowing the building blocks that support your actions and words can become a guide for improved communication and interaction. For example, if one of my goals is to visit one classroom every day, having that target in writing and rereading it weekly helps me keep that goal in focus. What I have come to learn is that having professional and personal goals and short- and long-term goals is crucial to achieving success. I've also learned that I need to write down my goals because they become more real that way. I can refer back to them as the year progresses. I can reread them; they don't fade away once the busy year begins. Trusting your memory can lead to your forgetting goals and responsibilities, resulting in what I call, "last-minute-fix-up leadership."

The approach I take in this book is that goals need to be set by those who are most involved in achieving them. That's the rationale behind spending intensive time in the summer on school improvement goals with department chairs.

Setting goals for yourself is just as important, and it's a good way to explore starting your school year.

Your Professional/Personal Goals Can Define Your School's Culture

Professional/personal goals require reflection on your hopes for the year. Besides questions that address school issues, you must reflect on your life outside of work. Keeping your life well-rounded is important. Burnout is very real in our profession and usually occurs when your school life devours your personal life.

As principal, you will feel the need to focus all your physical, emotional, and mental energies on the needs of students, staff, and parents. Administrators often work in excess of 70 hours per week. It's critical to learn balance. Make sure that you don't neglect your own needs, or you will burn out quickly. Exercise, spend time with your family and friends, eat healthy foods, go to movies and sports events—in other words, cultivate what makes you a happy and complete person. Most principals who have done the job for more than eight years have learned how to balance leadership with their lives beyond school.

New principals will struggle to find that balance. What I learned to do was to compartmentalize my life. While I'm at school, students, staff, and parents are my total focus. To avoid allowing the job to smother me, I push school issues out of my mind when I'm home with my family. Although it's tough, you'll need to accept that there are not enough hours in a day to complete everything, but do make sure that the crucial issues have been addressed before you leave school. Then go home and enjoy your family. Sometimes, emergencies, such as the police calling because an alarm has gone off or a door is unlocked, will reach into your home life. These are infrequent, but they will need your attention.

While balance is important for you, it's also important for your staff. I've hired new teachers who believe that they can impress me if they arrive at school at 6:30 a.m. and work as late as 9 p.m. If you see this happening in your school, I strongly suggest that you speak to these teachers and encourage them to cut back. We all can work long hours; the key is to structure time so it's used efficiently. New teachers who work incredibly long hours burn out quickly and often leave the profession. Setting and meeting your own personal goals can prevent you from losing balance and give you the insight to help teachers find the balance that leads them away from overplanning and poor time management to renewing themselves both physically and emotionally. Refreshed teachers with rich personal lives tend to be more effective teachers.

Ten Questions to Help You Set Goals

The ten questions below can help you set professional/personal goals. As you reflect on them, be honest. Write down your responses, and revisit them at least once a week during the year.

1. What are three words that describe how I want staff to perceive me?

2. What is my goal for returning correspondence to staff and the central office?

3. Which three professional development books will I read this year?

4. How can I improve my public speaking skills? List two areas of improvement.

5. How many classrooms will I visit each month?

6. How can I make lasting connections with our surrounding community?

7. How can I assure that our school improvement efforts move forward?

8. Which one personal hobby do I most want to pursue?

9. What will I do for my personal fitness and health?

10. About how much time do I spend with family and friends? Do I need to increase the amount, and how can I accomplish this?

Setting and continually revisiting your professional/personal goals is your insurance policy for maintaining the balance between your school and personal life. In addition, your goals will keep you in touch with your long-term responsibilities and help you build a positive and productive school community.

Beyond Professional/Personal Goals: Formulating School Goals to Start Your Year

Districts vary in how they expect principals to formulate their goals. Some districts have set categories for schools to build their goals within. If your district has set categories, it can be helpful to view how other principals have formatted and written their goals or how your predecessor did it. On the other hand, I've also constructed goals with no set criteria. As you gain more experience with the job, the latter is fine, but it can be challenging for a new principal. It takes time to see the larger picture, especially when you're engulfed by the present. This section presents categories to use to build school goals, questions to ask, and examples of goals for administrators to set. (See Appendix E, p. 168, for examples of goals I've created and presented to large and small groups. Review these before you formulate your own.)

A principal's goals should focus internally on the school and externally on how the school connects with its parents and community. When I was a new principal, I felt pressure from myself to create many goals. My thinking was that more goals would impress the central office. What I've learned is that having fewer goals and accomplishing them is always better than having many goals that fade away throughout the year.

What makes a goal achievable? A goal should be specific, measurable, attainable, realistic, and have a time frame for completion. (See Chapter 3 for more about setting goals.) A goal such as increasing staff morale is vague. However, it could be made more specific and measurable by surveying staff. A survey enables you to develop actions based on the data and review them over the course of the year.

What kind of information do I use to build goals? If you're a new principal in an established school or a school that hasn't performed well in the past, make sure you look at existing data to build goals. This can be data from standardized tests, which would include NCLB (No Child Left Behind) performance, survey data, personal reflections on summer school-improvement planning with department chairs, and/or conversations with a central office staff member. One thing is consistent in American public schools: they all have some type of performance data based on state testing and NCLB, and that's a good starting point for goal setting.

Many schools won't have good survey data. If yours doesn't, then creating and giving several surveys throughout the year may be a useful goal. Surveys can be used to collect staff feedback on current programs or to gauge interest in new ones. If your school has given surveys in the past, it is worth looking at the data to see whether the survey was done annually. If a survey has been given yearly, there should be longitudinal data that speaks to changes over time. Such a survey may be worth continuing. I once worked in a school that gave the same survey every year. The questions dealt with staff perceptions of how well the school functioned, so I had the luxury of comparing current data to past data.

Finally, the reality is that you may be told what your goals are. It's happened to me and will probably happen to you at some time. It's not an effective or inclusive method of doing things, but you may need to go along with it just the same. I personally don't feel one can grow when told what to achieve. We are best motivated when we set our own goals or we set them through conversations with a coach or a supervisor. Even if you have no choice in the goals set for your school, most likely you will have the ability to add goals as long as they coincide with the larger agenda; I suggest doing that.

Support Achievement for All With Five Goal-Setting Categories

The five goal-setting categories are student achievement, instruction, leadership, community relations, and school safety. Like all goals, they are designed to build and enhance achievement and improvement for all. No matter what kinds of goals your school district requires you to implement, these five categories can be woven easily into those requirements because they support students, staff, and community.

In addition to explaining each category and offering ideas for you to try, I've included questions to help you focus on your school's specific needs. Posing questions, I find, can help you pinpoint areas and issues that can improve instruction, students' progress in all subjects, and the environment.

1. STUDENT ACHIEVEMENT

The overarching purpose for students' attending school is for them to improve as readers, writers, thinkers, and speakers in core and other subjects. In a time of government-mandated standards and high-stakes tests, student achievement is an even more critical area to consider. Departments, grade-level teams, and other administrators need to focus their energies on school improvement. As you focus on student achievement, make sure that the goals you and staff set through summer school-improvement planning match your goals for student achievement and professional study.

Questions to Help You Reflect on Student Achievement

- Will staff development initiatives need to take place to achieve my goals?
- Will I need to create a system that monitors student achievement?
- Which areas that affect students' achievement should be emphasized this year?

Student Achievement Ideas That Work

Sharing data with one another: Ask teachers on a team or in the same department to analyze performance-based data, including classroom-generated assessments and mandated standardized tests, and then adjust the curriculum to meet their students' needs.

Enrichment: Provide additional learning for students who can move forward in one or more subjects.

Monitor students who are not successful: Explore ways to identify students who struggle and how to craft intervention plans to help them move forward.

2. INSTRUCTION

Once you're past your first year as principal, it will be easier for you to set instructional goals because you will have developed a knowledge of your school's culture and needs. As a new principal, you might be asked to set goals in this area. Here are some helpful questions to explore.

Questions to Help You Reflect on Instruction

- What instructional initiatives does my school need?
- Which department chairs and team leaders can offer me advice on these goals?
- Since these goals will affect my staff, how can I make them inclusive?
- Can instructional goals support school-improvement plans that were worked on during the summer?

Instruction Ideas That Work

Curriculum mapping: Start a building-wide effort to organize curriculum into three areas: content covered, skills and strategies needed to learn content, and an assessment plan.

Pacing the curriculum: Ask teachers to work together to plan how much content will be covered. These plans continually need adjustments as student achievement changes.

Developing common language: Have teachers come to a consensus on the language they will use with students in reading and writing?

3. LEADERSHIP

Your goals should include ways to develop leadership abilities among your staff. Accomplishing this can be challenging, especially if you're a first-year principal, for you need confidence and a strong sense of self to focus on creating leadership opportunities for others. Personally, I see this as an obligation. The questions that follow can help you think of ways to expand the potential of other adults in your building.

Questions to Help You Reflect on Leadership

- How am I sharing responsibilities with my administrative team? With teachers? With office staff?
- What specific leadership opportunities and responsibilities can I identify and offer to staff who seek leadership roles?
- Have I discovered which challenges my assistants would like?
- Do my key instructional leaders understand my expectations?

Leadership Ideas That Work

Organize book studies: Invite teachers to volunteer to organize and run these studies. Support them by paying for books the groups want to study and by setting aside times for meetings during their contracted time. Ask teacher leaders to keep you abreast of their meetings. Make sure you join a book study group as a participating member. (See Appendix F, pp. 169–170, for more information on book study clubs.)

School Web site: Ask a group of five to six teachers to update your school regularly by posting the dates of athletic games, plays and your school's talent show, special parent events such as a book fair, and so on on the Web site. The group can work with your school tech person, if you have one.

4. COMMUNITY RELATIONS

Consider a stool with three legs: one leg represents students, a second leg represents teachers and staff, and the third leg represents parents and community. A three-legged stool can stand. However, if a stool lacks one leg, it will fall. I return to that analogy frequently, for it reminds me that these three areas require constant attention. As you forge parent and community relations, return to the list of questions below to ensure that you're continually strengthening that third leg.

Questions to Help You Reflect on Community Relations

- How am I involving parents in the life of the school?
- Am I working with teachers to show them ways they can communicate with parents and involve them with their children's learning?
- Am I teaming parent volunteers with teacher leaders?
- Do I communicate with community members about the school?
- Am I calling attention to excellence in the school through the local newspaper and television station?
- Am I involving students in community service?

Community Relationship Ideas That Work

Create a school newsletter: Organize a collaboration between a group of parents and teachers to gather news from you, and your school's Web site, and by attending key events and to communicate this information through a newsletter. Distribute it to parents, community leaders, and businesses.

Plan parent-teacher events: Involve parents, along with teachers and office staff, in organizing refreshments and student displays for two to three scheduled parent nights that your school hosts. In addition, this group of leaders can organize a family reading night or an ice cream social with poetry readings to bring parents into the school.

Spread good news: Work to build relationships with your local newspaper and television station so that you can celebrate all the excellent events that occur in your school and share them with your community.

Community service programs: Meet with parents and teachers to develop ways to involve students in helping your community. They can volunteer at a local nursing home, soup kitchen, animal shelter, hospital, or day-care center.

5. SCHOOL SAFETY

School safety is a topic that becomes more important each year. Parents, community members, students, and staff expect their school to be safe. If the perception exists among some groups that your school is unsafe, then school safety will most likely be the "hot topic" in your community. To ensure a safe school environment, new principals must understand the procedures for all safety systems; veterans should know the safety system and set goals to improve it annually.

Questions to Help You Reflect on School Safety

- How accessible to outsiders is my school during the day? Are numerous doors open, or is only one door open—the door that leads to the office?
- Is there a surveillance system to monitor access areas?
- What are the school's visitor procedures? Should they be reevaluated?
- Is administrator and teacher visibility in the halls an area that needs improvement?
- Are duty stations effectively and consistently covered? Are expectations written out so the staff understands each duty?
- Does the school have clear procedures regarding students being in the hall during class time? Do they include consistent student bathroom procedures?
- Is data being kept on student tardiness to class? How can this be improved?
- Have procedures been created for fire drills, high wind drills, and lockdowns?

Strangers in the Building

Communicate to all staff members that if they see a person without a visitor badge in the building, they should politely ask the person if they can be of assistance.

Sometimes people can bypass the office, especially if it's a busy day; these folks need to be taken to the office immediately.

If staff members see an unfamiliar and/or suspicious-looking person, they should immediately report the person to an administrator.

School Safety Ideas That Work

Establish school visitor procedures: Post signs that read, "Visitors, please report to the office." Some schools have a set person near the door to greet and check in visitors. This is impractical for small schools that don't have the dollars for this extra staff member. I suggest that you limit visits to legal guardians or to people who have arranged beforehand to visit the school. Each visitor should sign in with one of the school secretaries and obtain and wear a visitor's badge. Parents shouldn't interrupt classes: defuse unexpected visits by angry parents by meeting with them immediately. A parent can leave a message with the secretary asking the teacher to call or e-mail.

> ### Support for Discipline
>
> **Marvin Marshall's book, *Discipline Without Stress, Punishments or Rewards,* is an excellent text to study. It offers ideas for proactively addressing discipline issues. If discipline and behavior issues persist, you might consider having a safety audit that involves local law enforcement officers and parents. This audit can help you pinpoint specific areas of concern and ultimately improve your school's safety.**

Monitor student office referrals: Maintain a record of the number of referrals for disciplinary action you're receiving and the number of suspensions teachers are giving. This data can tell you a great deal about student behavior and class disruptions. If teachers manage classes well, then referrals and suspensions should diminish from year to year. Reviewing last year's suspension and office-referral data can help you set goals for creating a safe school environment. Disruptions such as fights, excessive arguing, shoving, and constant talk can affect the safety of your students. You can address these issues at the start of the year with a workshop for staff on ways to deal with unproductive, negative student behavior.

Now That You've Established Goals, What's Next?

Share your list of goals with your staff at a faculty meeting. Once that's done, you can invite departments or grade-level teams to construct and share their own goals. (See Appendix G, p. 171, for the 2004–2005 goals I presented to my staff and the central office at an administrative retreat.) When you, other administrators, faculty, and staff develop and share your goals, you'll discover that you all share many in common such as improving instruction and discipline, and better communication.

This process shows teachers and staff that you are part of their community; you'll also build trust and a bonded team. Once a set of goals has been developed, it's time for you and your staff to construct a meaningful mission statement.

Merging onto the Mission Statement Highway

"A year from now you will wish you had started today." These words drive my beliefs about mission statements. Invest time early in the school year on your mission statement, and it will pay dividends by focusing staff on their purposes as educators. Moreover, when you create an inclusive process, your staff values the mission statement and uses it as a directional compass for your school.

Whether you're a first-time principal, you're new to a building, or you're starting a new school, collaborating with staff to create or revise a mission statement is an opportunity for you to build trust, vision, and commitment through shared work and beliefs. I've noticed that both new and experienced principals often don't view working on a mission statement as a high priority when they're opening a building. As I mentioned before, I've opened a new school and am aware of the stresses and time constraints administrators face to prepare a school and open its doors for the first time. However, a mission statement contains staff members' beliefs as well as what they hope to become. That's too powerful to be neglected.

Guidelines for Writing Mission Statements

A successful mission statement should do the following:
- Clearly state your school's purpose. Word choice is important. Be specific because vague and general words provide little meaning.
- Connect the ideas stated with specific practices at your school.
- Avoid being too wordy. Parents should grasp the statement's meaning easily. Three to seven sentences can do the job.
- Include staff, administration, and even parents and students in the process. Mission statements should be "we" statements, not "me" statements.
- Be revisited and reread frequently. Otherwise, it will be forgotten as the school year unfolds.

Leadership Tip:
Seeking Input

The first time I led my staff through the process of creating a mission statement, I tried to accomplish too much too quickly. Involving staff, parents, and students does slow things down. However, the results are worth the time: you will produce a mission statement with guiding goals that all support because they had a voice in creating it. Moreover, gathering the ideas of all school community members ensures that your school develops a mission statement that represents their beliefs and goals. Since no school exists in isolation from a community, it's important to seek their input.

The five guidelines I offer below can support a new or a veteran principal. As you read and consider these suggestions, reflect on your current situation and how the ideas can assist you in developing a new mission statement or in revising an existing one. Continue to reflect on these suggestions as you and your staff brainstorm ideas for your mission statement, while you compose a draft, and after you revise your draft. The process of reflection will focus you and your staff on the issues that you're wrestling with—and that you'll eventually have to agree upon.

1. GETTING STARTED

The following two questions should drive this beginning stage:

- Who should I involve in the process?
- How do I initiate the process?

The more representation you have from different groups, the easier it will be to build trust, commitment, and broad support for the mission statement. Since community groups often use a school in the evening and on weekends, involving representatives from these groups sends the message that you value their input and the activities they bring to your school. The central office, parents, and staff can also recommend community members to include. Recruit student representatives from among student government leaders and parent representatives by calling for volunteers in the school newsletter or your parent advisory group. Ask for staff volunteers through e-mail invitations or by extending an invitation during your first faculty meeting if your school has started already. (Note: It helps to have an even number on the drafting committee so the tasks can be divided among pairs or groups of four.)

Set aside about 60 minutes for the initial meeting. Discuss questions that raise everyone's awareness of key issues. Then form smaller groups to brainstorm the issues. Circulate among the groups as they work. After about 20 minutes, ask groups to share their ideas and then talk about their ideas. Jot down the main points raised in these discussions on chart paper. Some of following key points should arise:

- Continually improving student learning
- Valuing teachers and the teaching profession
- Supporting parents
- Involving the community in school life

Now that everyone's on board, you'll want to set a day and time for the second meeting. It's best not to let too much time pass between meetings, so you can maintain the momentum and enthusiasm generated by the first meeting. I recommend that you set and announce the time for the next meeting at the end of each completed meeting so you don't overwhelm group members with a list of upcoming dates.

2. SETTING REASONABLE TIME FRAMES

After the first meeting, you'll probably need four to five more one-hour meetings to collaborate on and compose a working draft of your mission statement.

Second meeting: I jigsaw questions by asking each group to choose one question that I've written down on a deck of index cards. Each group discusses its question for about 15 minutes, and then makes a presentation to everyone. After each presentation, anyone can add his or her take on the issue. Jigsawing not only moves the process forward, but it also reinforces a teaching strategy I hope faculty will bring to their classes.

Sample Jigsawing Questions

- **What does it mean to have satisfied parents? How can the school gauge satisfaction?**
- **Should we weave a commitment into the statement that calls for continual improvement, and if so, why?**
- **What do we want to instill in our students? What do we want them to remember from their experiences at our school?**
- **How can the community support our school?**

Third meeting: Hang the charts from the initial meeting around the room, and review the key issues. Call for new ideas, and jot these down too.

On the chalkboard, write the three questions below. They will help the group integrate ideas that emerge from the opening discussion.

- Who are we?
- What do and should we do?
- What do we value?

Invite small groups to use details from the charts to respond to these queries. Note their responses on chart paper.

Fourth meeting: Hang and review the charts with the responses to the three questions from the previous meeting. Then invite smaller groups to brainstorm a list of ideas they would like to see in the school's mission statement. As groups share their ideas, add any new thoughts that surface to their list of ideas. Ask your secretary to collate and type these ideas from the third and fourth meetings.

Final meeting: Distribute the typed list of ideas from the previous meetings. Hang all the charts so they are available as resources too. On the chalkboard or chart paper, write the following criteria to guide members as they compose a draft:

A. Make statements clear, specific, and easy to understand.
B. Use the word *we*.
C. State whom your school serves.
D. State how the school intends to prepare students for the future.
E. Describe what you value and hope to achieve.

Hold an open discussion, and then have smaller groups brainstorm details. Establish categories that correspond to letters from the above list. Record brainstormed ideas on chart paper under the applicable category.

3. SHARING THE FIRST DRAFT

Share the working draft with members of your school's community, and ask for feedback. Include the following groups:

- Staff members during a faculty meeting or during team planning periods
- Parent-advisory group members
- All student government officers
- Community members (via your school Web site or newsletter)

Remember, the more feedback you receive, the more inclusive the process will be—and the more commitment to the mission statement you will build. Therefore, encourage everyone to suggest changes. Then convene the committee and collaborate to make final adjustments. If there are many adjustments, invite the entire community to review the revised draft.

Examples of Excellent Mission Statements

You may find it helpful to read examples of other school's mission statements before drafting your own. It's important to clarify that these are examples, and that the committee needs to draft a mission statement that fits its school. Be up front with committee members and admit that it's tempting to copy all or part of another school's mission statement. However, since each school's population and culture differ widely, that's not an option.

If my committee wants to review other mission statements, I do this in an additional meeting.

You can use the examples that follow or collect them from other schools' Web sites.

- The mission of our school is to graduate students as contributing members of society, tolerant of others, empowered to shape their future using knowledge and skills developed in partnership with students, family, community, business, and government, with a safe environment.

- The mission of our school is to provide each student with a diverse education in a safe, supportive environment that promotes self-discipline, motivation, and excellence in learning. Our school team joins the parents and community to assist the students in developing skills to become independent and self-sufficient adults who will succeed and contribute responsibly in a global community.

- Our mission is to sustain a safe, nurturing environment in which the entire learning community addresses the unique needs of early adolescents and collaborates freely to ensure every student develops confidence, competence, and independent capacity through a rigorous curriculum and excellent instruction.

4. INTEGRATING YOUR MISSION STATEMENT INTO SCHOOL LIFE

For me, figuring out how to integrate the mission statement into the life of the school is a challenging and critical component of the process. I pose this problem to staff, parents, and committee members, for they share the responsibility for communicating the statement to the entire school community. Here are some suggestions I've collected and used:

- Print the mission statement for all staff members to post in their classrooms. Encourage them to review it with students.
- Place framed copies of the statement in your office and the main office and in central parts of the school, such as the library and cafeteria.
- Refer to the mission statement at special functions and faculty meetings.
- Remind students of parts of the mission statement in daily announcements. For example, once a week I read part of our mission statement as part of my daily announcements. This keeps these key ideas on the front burner and exposes all staff and students to our set of beliefs.

5. READING, REVIEWING, AND REVISING THE MISSION STATEMENT

A mission statement should be a vital, living document that you and the school community revisit again and again. Time will change aspects of your school's life: Teachers retire and new people replace them. You and your staff add new programs, discard some old ones, and adjust others. The superintendent may add additional grade levels or take some away. To remain real, relevant, and supportive, your mission statement will need continual adjustment. Again, the key always will be to include members from every group.

At the close of each school year, I revisit the mission statement with my staff as one of our end-of-the-year activities. We read and discuss it, but even more important, we ask ourselves if we are accomplishing our mission.

Continue to Think About . . .

This chapter has addressed several key points that can help a new or veteran principal create personal and school goals and mission statements. Key to these efforts is having a plan and methodically moving forward. Nothing effectively occurs if winging it is the method of operation. Good teachers always have a plan; so should effective principals.

If you've successfully gone through the processes in this chapter, you've begun to demonstrate your style without directly speaking to it. Recognize that how you foster and lead these initiatives sends a message to your staff, students, parents, and the community about what you value. This is a powerful form of leadership: leadership by example.

Before you continue reading, consider the following questions, reflect on them, and revisit them frequently:

- What schedule should I establish to review my personal and school goals?
- What can I do to make sure departments do not lose focus of their goals?
- How will I champion our collectively developed school mission?
- How do I make sure that our mission is a focal point of everything we do?

Chapter 3

School-Wide Improvement:

Making the Most of Faculty, Team, and Department Meetings

• • •

You can have brilliant ideas, but if you can't get them across, your ideas won't get you anywhere.

- Lee Iacocca

On a day in mid-August several years ago, I was sitting in my office, poring over the end-of-summer work-week schedule for staff and trying to figure out what to say at my first faculty meeting. Opening meetings can be upbeat and set the stage for a successful start, or they can set a negative tone. I can recall feeling very unsure and overwhelmed. The reality of my job was settling in fast. When I took the position, I had felt confident about what I would do and even what I would say at the opening meeting. But now I felt the pressure. Was I on target with what I had needed to accomplish during July up until now? The basic work was done. With the support of teachers and my assistants, I had staffed the school, completed teacher and student schedules, and developed handbooks for teachers, parents, and students. In addition, all the necessary class supplies had been ordered.

I had a head full of ideas of what to say to the staff at our first official meeting. What gave me pause was that if I came on too strong, I might alienate some staff; if I appeared too weak, I might do the same. The school was new, therefore, all procedures would be new. That was both exciting and nerve-wracking. The worst scenario was that the job would control me. I would lose sight of the big picture, as well as of my ideas and passion, and focus on day-to-day survival, just trying to make it to the weekend.

On that day in mid-August, I realized that it was up to me to create an environment where I could effectively lead. I could have great ideas. I could elicit support and create an environment that honored input and collaboration. Or I could become the principal who loses his grip on leadership and commitment to children and staff. My motivation to make things work was high, but I knew that the path would have downturns and obstacles and that school community members could be unforgiving at times. I recalled times when my friends and I would criticize the principals of our schools. It was easy to do—and enjoyable at times, especially since we didn't have the job. As a principal, I accepted the reality that if the school excelled, I would have some responsibility for that. Conversely, if things didn't go well, many would blame me.

As I checked the lock on the last door that mid-August day, I felt confused and anxious about the next few weeks. Negative voices kept resurfacing. I couldn't suppress the feeling that some graduate classes hadn't prepared me for what I'd been doing since early July. I needed a mentor to guide me, but there was no one to call upon.

What got me through those stressful weeks? The threefold support that safely navigated me through that time was my detailed planning, interactions with staff, and my commitment to educating all children. Working hard, seeking counsel from my staff and assistants, and planning helped to focus my energy on the first week of teacher meetings.

In this chapter, you'll see how planning for the five initiatives listed below can diminish those negative voices all principals sometimes hear.

● Organize a work-week schedule for when new and veteran staff return.

● Prepare what you plan to say at the first faculty meeting of the year.

● Map out administrative and faculty meetings throughout the rest of the year.

● Collaborate with staff to create themes that can add purpose to meetings.

● Support teams and departments as they set goals for improving students' achievement.

As you plan these initiatives, make sure you seek advice from teachers, staff, and your assistants as you build consensus.

1. Summer Work Week for Staff: Build Community When Staff Returns

The first week back for teachers is an exciting time. They feel energized about the coming year, but they also may be concerned that their work-week schedule will be clogged with meetings. I've found it best to keep the first week as open for teachers as possible. Consider the following important items as you plan your work-week schedule:

● Be aware of the specific times of events scheduled by the central office. The central office will often have a morning for a system-wide ceremony and financial fair. It may also require certain staff for in-services.

● If your school is not new, look at the previous year's schedule. If it looks good (meaning teacher work time is adequate), you may want to reuse it. If the schedule has very little teacher work time and is bogged down with meetings, consider revising it.

Leadership Tip:
Choose a Consensus-Building Leadership Style

I've found that some principals consistently make top-down decisions and lead through fear and intimidation. This leadership style is ineffective. It destroys trust, builds anger and frustration, and doesn't develop a community of learners among teachers who care about one another, their students, and their school. I urge you to walk the path of what I consider to be effective leadership. On this path, you'll communicate your vision and call for consensus building on academic and personnel issues. You'll build trust between you and other administrators and among staff, along with the commitment to a vision and goals that all school community members develop.

- If this is your first year at a school, mail a welcoming and newsy letter that introduces you to all staff. Do this by the middle of July. Then, at least two weeks before the staff returns, send a second letter to discuss the work week before school opens and include a schedule for that week. This letter sets the stage for when staff returns. (See Appendix H, pp. 172–174, for examples of welcome-back letters.) Your staff will appreciate these letters.

- In the schedule, include two faculty meetings for the work week, one on the first day back and the other on the last day of the work week. Elementary schools will need time for grade-level and content-area meetings. Middle schools and high schools with teams or departments will need scheduled meeting times for those groups. Finally, if the school has a lead-teacher structure, set a date to meet with them.

- Also, allow adequate time in the work-week schedules for teachers to work in their rooms; they will appreciate your consideration. No teacher likes to feel that meetings during the week are taking him or her from time needed in the classroom.

- Place copies of the schedule for the work week on the workroom table and in the front office. Even though the schedules were mailed earlier, putting extra copies in visible areas will be appreciated.

2. Making That First Meeting Top-Notch

Planning the agenda and your remarks for the first faculty meeting can set the tone for the opening weeks of school. Part of my planning and thinking about this all-important meeting includes gathering suggestions and advice from my assistants and setting aside time to anticipate questions the staff might pose. Then I prepare responses. In addition, I keep paper on my desk so I can jot down ideas that I can include in my opening remarks to staff.

Planning the Agenda

Discuss the meeting with your assistants. Set aside time to meet with them and your deans to anticipate questions the staff might ask during the meeting. A discussion with your administrative team can generate questions such as those listed below. Prior to the first faculty meeting, these discussions can help the new and veteran administrator feel comfortable about fielding questions.

- What is our meeting schedule for the year?
- How are we doing duties? Can we have a duty-free lunch?
- Since you're the new principal, will I have to hand in lesson plans?
- Do you conduct announced or unannounced observations?
- Where do kids who don't have schedules report the first day?

It's interesting to note that every time I've started a new position, these five questions always arise. Some of them result from the fear of change, such as conducting unannounced teacher observations. Others tend to be personal and relate to time commitments and convenience, such as the number of meetings or the level of detail required in lesson plans. Preparation will enable you to give calm and thoughtful replies to queries, so take time to formulate answers to these anticipated questions. An inaccurate response, especially one about lesson plans, can make your life difficult in the future. Carefully think about how you want to answer the question; someone will ask it.

I've purposely left out "big picture" types of questions such as *What is your vision for the school?* or instructional-related questions such as *How can we better integrate writing into all subjects?*. These are too vast to bring up at opening meetings and addressing them quickly and without depth can cause misunderstandings about your beliefs and instructional goals.

If you're coming into an established school, find out the previous principal's expectations for planning. If you're opening a new school, have an understanding of how other principals in your system or district communicate planning expectations. I've always believed that effective planning leads to more effective teaching. However, if the school you enter hasn't had any planning expectations and is an effective school, a quick decision to require lesson planning may not be in your best interest. Such a mandate can provoke anger among teachers over extra work and reduce their confidence in you. This doesn't mean that planning in such a school wouldn't be beneficial, but how you go about it and when you initiate the change requires thought on your part—and taking the time to build a consensus.

Organizing the Meeting

The day of the first meeting has arrived. It's natural to be nervous, but being prepared can diminish your anxiety. The tips discussed below can help you organize a successful first meeting.

Set the stage: Plan to have refreshments at the meeting. Your staff will enjoy socializing over food; it's a great icebreaker. Also, before the meeting, I like to set flowers on each table. Then I tape an index card that reads, "You Won the Flowers!" underneath a randomly selected chair at each table. Giving away these flowers will be the closing activity for the meeting.

Before you speak, circulate around the room. It gives a bad impression if you're seen speaking with only a few people. Finally, make sure you have a clear idea in your mind of how long you want this preliminary part of the meeting to be.

Effective Icebreakers for Meetings

Icebreakers can be creative and enjoyable. If done right, they set a relaxing tone for the meeting. Each activity is short, simple to do, and should be well received by staff.

Form a Line Activity: Have staff line up in the room based on years of experience. This always makes for humorous conversations. Point out how beneficial it is to the school and students to have such a wealth of experience in the school.

Code for Candy Activity: Place candy in a container on the tables where staff are sitting. Tell them to choose the type of candy they want, and ask them to keep their wrappers. The wrappers will tell teachers what to share with their colleagues. Then place the "Code for Candy" like the one that follows on an overhead projector.

  Snickers: one of your favorite movies
  Milky Way: your worst customer-service experience
  Three Musketeers: your number of years in education
  Dark Milky Way: wild card—say anything you want
  No Candy: something special you did this summer

I find that this game helps break the ice for those who are unsure about what they want to share with others.

Pull From the Shoebox Activity: This is an excellent activity for staff who know each other and have a solid rapport with administration. A principal who is new to the school should not do this activity. Each staff member draws a slip of paper from a shoebox and then shares his or her response with the rest of the group. Make sure you have enough slips for each staff member. Place the following three choices in the shoe box:

  1. A hidden talent you have
  2. Expectations for the meeting today
  3. A secret vice or peeve

Interesting Fact Activity: While staff members enjoy the refreshments, ask them to write down an interesting fact about themselves and place it in a box. For instance, they might share a hobby or an unusual skill. To begin the meeting, pull a fact out of the box, read it, and allow staff to guess who it is. Continue until all the facts have been revealed.

When you speak, thank those who helped you over the summer. Make a list of people you want to thank; it's embarrassing to forget important people. Personalize this recognition by giving brief but specific examples of what each person did. Plan introductions that honor staff and make them feel comfortable. There are various ways to introduce staff. I like to begin by introducing new staff members, and if the group is small, I say a few words about each one. Putting new staff on the spot and having them introduce themselves in front of the entire faculty can be embarrassing or unnerving to some. If the group of new staff is large, write down their names on an index card along with a key point you would like to make about each one, such as hometown, past work experiences, or college attended. Keep your comments about them brief.

At this point, let me caution you to avoid connecting every new member with a sports team by saying, "Here's Susan. She's from Miami. Her favorite colors are orange and blue, and she thinks the Dolphins will win it all next year." These kinds of introductions can offend staff members who have no interest in sports and give a one-sided, insensitive impression of you that may take a long time to reverse.

The box on the previous page provides some icebreakers that my staff members have enjoyed. If one or two people don't want to participate, let them make that choice. But be sure to chat with them privately to find out what motivated them to make this decision.

Make your opening speech a winner: Since the staff wants to get on with their day, I don't suggest long speeches at this meeting. And don't read your speech. Have a general idea of what you want to cover and jot down key points on an index card. Reading a speech can make you appear stiff and gives the impression that you don't know details well enough to recall them. Be upbeat, energetic, and positive. I enjoy talking about my summer, interjecting a funny story, and finally communicating the picture for what I hope the year will be. In my current school, I focus on working together, honoring and respecting established traditions, and communicating that the journey toward excellence takes time. Again, laying out detailed initiatives for the year should not be done at this opening meeting.

Give an overview of the work week and plan duty assignments, and make sure that all staff members have a schedule for the week. If you're the new principal in an established school, it's important to find out how duties were assigned the previous year.

Unless there were glaring problems, I would keep duties the same. Nothing will ruin the first meeting more than changing duty assignments; teachers will be angry, and negative talk can become the focal point. The key is to make your duty roster goal coincide with teachers' expectations.

If the school is new, find out how other schools in your system or district handle duties. Ask questions such as the following:

- Do all schools in the district have duty-free lunches?
- Does the administration assign duties or do grade-level teams create their own duty rosters?

Weave in other key speakers: To stay within the time parameters you've established, suggest time limits for other speakers. Your assistant principals, a guidance counselor, the front office secretary, the school resource teacher, and the parent advisory group president might want a few minutes to speak to the staff. I offer them that option. However, I'm respectful if anyone prefers not to speak, and I make their announcements based on notes they provide to me.

End on an upbeat note: I like to save special staff recognitions for the end of the first meeting. Recognitions might be given for such things as completing a master's degree or attending a workshop or special training class. My primary goal is to set the stage for a successful week and school year. Before closing the meeting, I always let the staff know that on the faculty meeting on Friday, I'll review the schedule for the students' first day of school.

Always ensure that your staff leaves the meeting feeling energized and with the sense that you have worked hard to set aside unscheduled times in the work week so teachers can prepare their rooms and meet with colleagues. Finally, tell the staff to look under their chairs for a card, and explain that if they've found one, they've won the flowers on their table. Congratulate the winners, thank everyone for a great meeting, and send the group on its way.

Leadership Tip:
Good News Spreads Quickly

If your faculty meetings are productive and focus on supporting teaching practices and students' learning, your staff will enjoy them, participate fully, and the buzz about the meetings will be positive. To accomplish this, I suggest that three days prior to each meeting you send administrative notes that cover such things as schedule changes, upcoming visitors and due dates for reports and committee results to staff so that you can dedicate each meeting to curriculum and instruction. Remember, meetings are a fact of school life. How you run them and the agendas you propose are areas to attend to, whether you're a new principal or a veteran.

Keep the second meeting of work week short and focused: When I opened a new school, I used our second and final faculty meeting of the work week to review, in detail, the first-day-of-school procedures for students and staff. (See Appendix I, pp. 175–177 for an example.) Since the school was new, I carefully discussed the movement of students with staff, and together we brainstormed solutions to potential glitches that my assistant and I thought might arise.

In an established school, returning staff will most likely know their roles on the first day of school. First, discuss how the first day went the previous year with an assistant and any department chairs or team leaders who were there. Make adjustments in the schedule, and present them to the faculty for discussion. Meet with new teachers separately and let veterans work in their classrooms.

In addition to developing and reviewing smooth first-day procedures, I use this last meeting of work week as an opportunity to reflect on the week and to gear up staff for the opening day. Start by sharing a funny event that occurred during the week or a personal story. Encourage others to share an upbeat anecdote. Close by expressing your confidence that by working together, the opening day and first week will more than meet everyone's expectations because of the hard work and thoughtful communication you've observed.

3. Make the Most of Faculty Meetings Throughout the Year

Traditionally, the purpose of faculty meetings has been to disseminate information; newer models focus on professional development. Faculty meetings should deal with teaching and learning with the goal of improving student achievement and closing learning gaps. I recommend that you use faculty meetings to look at data, to share instructional successes, and/or to work on school-wide initiatives such as a Web site, curriculum mapping, and reading initiatives. Making this happen can be a challenge, but you have the key role in setting the tone and agenda for faculty meetings. If your goal is to make meetings significantly different from past years, this will take time. But it will be time well spent, especially if your aim is to build a professional learning community whose purpose is to support teachers and parents and to meet the learning needs of all students.

Considering the two questions and my commentary below can help you make every faculty meeting an effective one.

● **If the school is new, what type of schedule do you want to establish for faculty meetings?**

Even though new schools may not have set ways of doing things, it's advisable to speak to another principal in your system to find out about his or her school's faculty meeting schedule. If the new principal introduces a meeting schedule that contains more meetings than other schools in the system have, faculty may resent it. If as the new administrator you're unsure of what schedule to establish, I suggest meeting once each month. An easy way to do this is to hold meetings on the third Thursday of each month, either before or after school. Fix the day and time for the year so your staff can mesh their out-of-school commitments with meeting days.

Avoid having staff vote on the day or time they want to meet as a faculty; believe me, no staff can reach consensus on a date and time. Set the date and accept that things will come up that will cause staff members to miss a meeting once in a while. Rarely will attendance be 100 percent.

- **If you're the new principal at an established school, are you aware of the other meetings that take place in the school?**

Spend some time finding out what meetings have been part of the school's routine, such as faculty meetings, grade-level meetings, department meetings, and team meetings. Even if you don't fully agree with the established meeting times, I suggest starting the year using similar or identical schedules. After the first two to three meetings, survey teachers to gather feedback on how they would like to adjust meeting times. Always strive for consensus— knowing you will rarely achieve full consensus. I urge you to meet with teachers who fall out of the loop and try to meet their needs regarding times or simply excuse them if they can't make a meeting. Moreover, listening to teachers and allowing them to vent is often all they need as long as you help them understand the reasoning behind your decisions.

Meeting Guidelines That Work

The effective principal will be up-front with her expectations during meetings early in the year. Communicating guidelines about meeting procedures can help the staff better understand the style of the principal as well as the purpose of meetings.

As a new principal, review your meeting procedures in the smaller meetings you hold during the first week that the staff is back. This is not a topic for the first faculty meeting; however, information on meeting procedures can be introduced at grade-level meetings, team meetings, or department meetings. These guidelines affirm your desire for professional meetings that honor opinions, encourage all to participate, and explore topics that can improve teaching and students' learning. I communicate to each group that I want to minimize the number of meetings and the amount of time they take. To do so, meetings need to be organized and remain within scheduled time limits. By being aware of the basic procedures, meeting participants will always be more effective and efficient.

It's important for a principal to develop a personal system for organizing meetings. The following list proposes some helpful meeting protocols for you to reflect on and adapt to your needs:

- Send out the agenda two to three days before the meeting.
- Give staff members an opportunity to contribute to the agenda.
- Encourage members to be punctual.

- Start the meeting on time.
- Urge participants to listen actively and participate.
- Discourage side conversations.
- Come to the meeting with a willingness to build consensus.
- Value opinions: no one should be afraid of speaking up.
- Follow the agenda: keep the meeting on track.
- Set a time for the meeting to end-and honor it.
- Record the minutes and communicate them to staff in an e-mail or at the next meeting.

For any meeting that I'm responsible for, I state that I'll do my best to be true to my personal style. I've always made it a point to be clear with my staff about how I run meetings as well as my expectations for the participants. However, I'm also up-front about the fact that I don't want to dictate how other groups within the school run their meetings.

Leadership Tip: Thoughts on Meetings

Preparation for meetings is critical for a principal. For staff to value meetings, they need to feel their time in meetings is well spent. Organizing, planning, and creating an agenda, and then following it will increase effectiveness. Never assume that basic procedures for meetings will become part of your school culture by presenting them once or by e-mailing them to staff. Most staff members will need time to learn this new way of running meetings, especially if your predecessor ran them differently. My suggestion is to print the meeting guidelines on the back of each agenda that you send out. This reinforces the importance of the guidelines and allows the staff to revisit them throughout the year.

The way in which you run meetings provides an opportunity to lead by example. The key is to continually demonstrate new and more efficient ways of running meetings to your staff and, at the same time, to remain patient. When you let your actions motivate staff slowly, you build trust and commitment toward you and the school. Forcing uniform procedures can build anger and distrust and accentuate negative attitudes and feelings among your staff. Let your actions motivate changes.

4. Annual Themes: Zoom In on Improving Learning

Now let's move our thinking toward how to create meetings that focus staff on professional study and teaching. When I was a new principal, I wanted to add learning and professional development to my faculty meetings, yet I faced the classic problem of how to do it. Unfortunately, during my first year, meetings came to mean disseminating information. What my staff and I needed were one or two themes that would be the guideposts, the beacons for our collective growth. A theme such as writing to improve reading can become the framework for each meeting. It can weave related teaching and learning ideas into one cloth—and it can determine our professional reading.

Choosing a theme for the year should be based on your school's needs. There are several ways to choose a theme: you can set it based on feedback from a survey or from consensus-building conversations with staff. Themes help focus you and the faculty on improving students' learning and achievement and on best-practice teaching.

I've used the following themes in my schools:

- Academic rigor
- Grading and assessments
- Lessons and interventions based on assessments
- Reading strategies and content-area learning
- Writing to learn across the curriculum
- Writing to improve reading comprehension
- Self-evaluation: teachers and students
- Planning units of study
- Cross-disciplinary units of study
- Independent free-choice reading
- Bringing a workshop approach to all subjects

Make sure the theme connects to all subjects. At your first learning-centered faculty meeting, discuss the theme's relevance to the school and brainstorm some subtopics. For example, the theme in my school one year was grading and assessment. My staff agreed on three subtopics: (1) to improve consistency in grading; (2) to connect grading to mastery of state standards; and (3) to study the connections between our existing grading system and student failure. Faculty members and my administrative team formed groups to focus on each of these subtopics. The groups committed to giving a presentation at each faculty meeting. In order to make effective presentations, each group met several times, gathered and studied data, and planned elements to share with their colleagues. In the presentations, they suggested articles for the entire faculty to read, shared current research, and reported successes with a new grading method we were trying.

Transforming faculty meetings into professional learning communities shifts the principal's job from planning all the activities and agenda items to reminding staff of their agreed-upon meeting responsibilities. The theme brings a common focus to professional reading, to discussions, to classroom practice, and to productive and research-based changes in students' learning. Listen for the moment that conversations on the theme start to move outside the meeting. When that happens, you're on the right track!

A theme can also provide the framework for small-group meetings that convene regularly. I think of it as the glue that holds the goals of the diverse groups in a building together.

Additional Meetings at Your School

Listed below are meetings that occur in almost all schools. Please review this list and the noted benefits. Then reflect on your responses to these questions: *Does your school have these group meetings? If so, what changes need to be made in them?* Halfway through the year and again close to the end of the year, poll your staff's reactions to these meetings and study their suggestions for improving them. Changes should always reflect the feedback and input of your staff so they recognize that you value and act upon their ideas.

Administrative meetings: This meeting group can consist of the administrators and guidance director. ***Benefit:*** Setting an established schedule to meet with your administrative team is a great way to increase communication, build relationships, troubleshoot, and discuss progress with school goals.

Committee meetings: Set up committees to explore issues or to meet needs, such as discipline, report card procedures, and homework policy. ***Benefit:*** Committees are an excellent way to involve staff in school decision making and to keep a school running smoothly. I've found that setting timelines for committees to reach conclusions is a great way to keep them focused and efficient; negotiate these timelines with each committee. When a committee has finished its task, its members can present their findings at a faculty meeting.

Curriculum meetings: These meetings are opportunities for teachers of a common subject, such as English, to meet and discuss curriculum goals. ***Benefit:*** Teachers can develop ways to improve content and instruction, and ways to differentiate learning tasks and meet students' needs. Curricular meetings should occur at least once a month. Ask a group member to take minutes of the meeting.

Team meetings: Many middle schools have teams of teachers who have common planning time. ***Benefit:*** Common planning time is a wonderful way for teachers to meet during the school day. These groups can discuss student issues and the goals they've set and disseminate important information. Teams should also record the minutes of their meetings.

Department meetings: Middle and high schools frequently form departments by subject. Traditionally, department meetings focus on curriculum and teaching practices. ***Benefit:*** Departments can continually evaluate the curriculum and their curriculum maps. They can also study best practices and link them to instruction and student achievement.

Keep in mind that the purpose of all meetings should be to set goals that support the students in your school by providing learning experiences that gently move them forward.

5. Department and Team Goal Setting Fosters Student Progress

To stimulate a discussion among departments and teams about goal setting, I once offered a business analogy that I knew my staff would balk at and find solid reasons for not adopting; I suggested that teams and departments set and meet monthly targets. Immediately, everyone pointed out, "We're not a business. We're a school."

One teacher noted, "There are human variables in a school that need consideration."

Another teacher said, "The central office always gives us our goals."

"Hmm," I replied. "Have you ever considered that our school might present goals that we've agreed upon to the central office?"

Silence. Several minutes of silence. Then I asked, "How do you feel when others impose goals on you?"

This query generated a lively discussion among the staff members. The heart of the matter was that they felt frustrated at being called professional and yet always being told what to do.

I sympathized with them and carefully explained that I had similar feelings when I taught a middle school reading-writing workshop. Like them, I wanted to have input into setting goals instead of receiving a list of mandated goals. At that time, it wasn't an option for me, but I told the teachers that I wanted it to be an option for them. Then I asked, "How do you feel about working together to create our own goals, provided that you and I are willing to monitor them?"

I wanted my staff to be proactive and not wait for others to tell them what to do and how to manage their classrooms. For me, change is best when it's made by those most affected by the change. Moreover, department and team planning should keep student learning and achievement in full view. Our meeting ended with positive results: teachers agreed to collaborate to set goals and submit them to the central office.

Departments, Teams, or Both?

Middle schools are unique, for most have grade-level teams and departments. Grade-level teams are the hallmark of elementary schools, while high schools have subject departments and department chairs. In my current middle school, grade-level teams set goals that relate to student achievement and failure, communication with parents, and home visits. Departments deal with curriculum and teaching practices. In schools that use only one of these two administrative groupings, all of these goals can be dealt with in one place.

I suggest that during the work week prior to the opening of school, teams and/or departments schedule two one-hour meetings to review the previous year's goals, to start the process of adjusting and changing them to fit the new annual theme, and to strive to meet the needs of students. At this time, one or both groups should set a meeting timeline for early fall, for the winter months, and for the spring. This provides the group members with opportunities to agree upon and write their goals by the first week in October; set them into motion by the end of October; and to review, adjust, and evaluate them over the remainder of the year.

Note that these groups meet during common planning times. If, however, your school contract allows for teachers to initiate this process the week before school work week, have them start then.

Let's Get Started: Tips for Writing Effective and Clear Goals

When setting goals, use the SMART structure. Goals should be *s*pecific, *m*easurable, *a*ttainable, *r*ealistic, and *t*imely. You can see the effectiveness of the SMART structure by using it to evaluate the two goals below.

● Our department is going to increase parental contact this year.

● On the last workday of each month, the members of each department (or team) will send postcards to ten parents. Our focus this year will be on recognizing students who have improved academic achievement and behavior each month. We will keep a record of the students recognized every month and give the list to our department chair, who will collate the lists and turn them over to Mr. Robb.

Clearly, the second goal follows the SMART guidelines. The first goal is not specific and would be tough to measure. Testing the improvement goals you set using the SMART structure ensures that the wording will be detailed, clear, and easy to measure.

Before groups start their discussion of goals and school improvement, give them a copy of the following three guidelines:

1. Reflect on last year's plan, and make an honest assessment of what worked and what can be improved.

2. Test your goals against the SMART structure.

3. Limit your plan to a half page to one page at the most.

Remember, good planning is about continual improvement; revisiting and evaluating last year's goals will help you and your staff frame positive and productive goals for the upcoming year. I suggest limiting goals to one page. Any more than that can become unachievable, overwhelming teachers and resulting in groups giving up on the process.

Questions that Encourage Discussion Among Teams and Departments

I find that offering questions for teams and departments to consider before their first meeting is an excellent way to stimulate discussion and debate. Questions such as those that follow can bring diverse ideas to the surface and prompt group members to deepen their reflection process as they continue to flesh out and fine-tune their goals. You'll notice that there are two kinds of questions: questions that encourage open discussion of what kinds of goals should be framed, and questions that start members thinking about ways to use goals in their teaching lives.

- Do we need new goals, or should we concentrate on completing last year's goals?
- Are some reading and learning strategies repeated too frequently? Are some not being used often enough?
- Are we leaving out key learning and reading strategies?
- Do we have too many or too few goals? What can we do about this?
- Should there be a minimum and maximum number of goals for each team or department? Should the number of goals vary? If so, why?
- Do our goals cover student improvement?
- Are we addressing how to support students who are failing?
- How can we make the wording of our goals more specific?
- Have our goals included ways to communicate with parents and caregivers?
- Do our goals fill one page or less? If not, how can we prioritize the goals to eliminate some?

- How can we keep these goals on the front burner and revisit them throughout the year?
- Should our meeting timelines be more specific?
- How will we communicate these goals to other staff? To administrators? To parents?

Your team leaders and your department chairs and their faculty can use these questions as a springboard for designing goals that can improve instruction, students' learning, and communication with parents.

Develop a Timeline for Your Improvement Plan

You play an important role in helping teams and/or departments develop specific goals for the year and setting a timeline that will keep teachers focused on implementing and evaluating their goals throughout the year. First, you'll have to decide whether all groups will create their own goals or whether you want to guide the process by selecting areas of common focus for the school. I recommend selecting two or three areas of focus. By doing so, you rally the entire school around specific goals. Having common goals can bond teams to one another as they share what's working and provide support and feedback for each other. For example, I might ask teams and/or departments to adopt the following two goals:

- Grade-level teams: Reduce student failures and increase parent contact.
- Department teams: Weave writing to learn into all subjects and into all assessments other than tests.

Teams and/or departments can also create two to three goals of their own. As I've already mentioned, if your school has only teams or only departments, then you'll need to integrate curricular and performance goals. In my school, setting goals for school-wide improvement emerges from my suggestions and from the specific needs that teams and departments observe.

The ideal time to initiate this process is during work week when students are not in school. Meet with teams and/or departments during the work week. During this week, I like to get together with faculty for a short, focused meeting to set common goals and to explain the SMART structure so they can use it to evaluate and revise the wording of the goal statements they create. I encourage groups to have candid dialogues, and I ask them to frame two additional goals by the end of two weeks. Setting this time frame ensures that the school will embark on implementing goals early in the year. Finally, I remind them that their list of goals should fit on a single page.

Ten Tips to Make Team and Department Goals Part of Your School's Culture

1. Publicly recognize goal attainment at faculty meetings, in your school newsletter, and on your Web site.

2. Laminate or frame goals, and ask each group member to keep them in a prominent place.

3. Have each department and team leader meet with you every month to access progress toward achieving their goals.

4. Send monthly e-mails reminding staff to focus on their goals and offering your assistance.

5. Invite department and team leaders to present their goals to your parent organization.

6. If you have a professional development day, set time aside for departments and teams to meet and evaluate progress toward achieving their goals.

7. Find an opportunity for a department or team leader to present the goal-setting process to other teachers.

8. Set a meeting with your team leaders and a separate one with department chairs near the end of the calendar year. Have each person give an overview of his or her goals, pointing out areas of success and ones they found challenging. Have the group offer feedback for moving forward those challenging goals.

9. Send a copy of your school's goals to your central office. Invite a central office staff member to a meeting and explain the process to him or her.

10. Challenge groups to find creative ways to let parents know about their goals.

Then everyone gathers at a full faculty meeting in September to share and discuss their goals. I want all groups to be aware of the planning and goals that have been established, for this builds community and enthusiasm for making progress and supporting one another. **Set up a midyear check point.** By the middle of the school year, plans for school improvement can begin to fade. To prevent this from happening, encourage teams to discuss their goals at all their meetings. Since you can't attend every meeting, you have to trust that these discussions are occurring. To keep groups on track, I do the following:

● At the start of the school year, I tell teams and departments that in the first week after winter break they will meet to discuss and update their plans, and that I always attend that meeting.

● During the fall, I remind teachers in monthly e-mails to revisit their goals.

● About two weeks prior to winter break, I remind teachers that I'll be meeting with them in January. (If your school is large and meeting with everyone becomes an issue of time, I suggest that you meet with two to three teams a day during their planning periods.) At this point, I also e-mail the questions below for teachers to reflect on, and I let them know that these questions will be discussed at the January meeting and at the end of the year.

● What goals have you achieved? Can you share evidence of goal achievement?

● Were your timelines effective? Do you need to adjust them?

● Which goals were the greatest challenge? Explain why.

● Which goals haven't been reached? What kind of support do you think you need to reach these goals?

● What can I do to assist your group to reach all its goals?

● What do you see as your greatest challenge during the second half of the school year, and why?

Note that these questions are specific and go beyond asking for a summary. From experience, I've found that being general can allow groups to avoid confronting important roadblocks and working to move past them. Once groups have adjusted their plans, I again encourage them to revisit and discuss their goals each time they meet.

Evaluate plans near the end of school. If your school has final faculty meetings, set aside time for groups to evaluate their goals as well as time for you to meet with department chairs and team leaders. You can also request that groups do this during common planning times about three weeks prior to the end of school. Before school closes for summer break, take time to celebrate all the success that the groups achieved. I like to have a breakfast with bagels, juice, and coffee and show teachers how their hard work translated into progress and improvement for our students.

I also require each team and department to submit a written report to me. I read these reports carefully during July and August and frame questions for teams to review and discuss when school begins again—questions that can help them refine this process and do all they can for students and their families. After several years of reading and reflecting on goal reports, I've developed ten tips that can make the journey of setting goals smoother and more productive.

I want you to see how team and/or department goals can shape your school's improvement. Also, you'll have developed a culture in which your faculty supports the goals because they worked hard to create and adjust them. Remember, great goals are worth little if they go into file folders and teachers never use them. Consider the tips listed in the box on page 75 and adjust them to your needs. They can ensure that the goal-creation process becomes part of your school's life and culture.

Examples of Team and Department Goals

Now, let's take a look at two real-life examples: a sixth-grade team's goals (Figure 3.1) and the goals of a Math Department for grades 6, 7, and 8 (Appendix J, p. 178). Note that the sixth-grade team, which includes teachers from all subjects, zooms in on dealing with students who are failing and provides detailed ways to reverse the failure cycle. The team was able to carry out this plan because it focused on an issue for that year. Once a team successfully deals with an issue, its problem-solving strategies become part of its culture, even as the team moves forward to tackle new goals.

Figure 3.1: Team 6 SMART Goals, 2005-2006

Student Failure

- Every two weeks during team meeting, students with D/F grades will be discussed. Students with multiple Fs or Ds will be put on a school improvement plan
- From 7:45 a.m. to 8:12 a.m., multiple F students will be in a designated class room for study hall. Students should attend daily Monday through Thursday.
- Interventions for students: if someone other than a teacher is providing the intervention, teachers need to be contacted for documentation. Please send this information to the team leader.

POSITIVE CONTACTS
- All students will be contacted by November.
- When data sheets are submitted, the team leader will document who was contacted.
- Teachers will still continue to contact parents after November goal is met. This information should be sent every Friday to the team leader for documentation.

STUDENT IMPROVEMENT FORMS
- Students with multiple Fs and Ds will have SIP filled out for them. Team will keep a weekly watch to document interventions.
- The team will meet/discuss with student and parent.
- Resolutions for teacher/student/parent will be listed (if they apply).
- Copies of plans will be sent to the team leader and the guidance center.

HOME VISITS
- Two are mandatory by county.
- In addition, by the end of the school year, teacher(s) will have made a visit to parent(s)/guardian of struggling students.
- Dates and times of home visits will be sent to the team leader on the last school day of each month.

Math Department goals for grades 6, 7, 8: The goals focused on monitoring the performance of all students, supporting those who needed scaffolding, and recognizing successful students as well as improvement in performance. Note that the math department strived for consistency of assessments, strong communication between grade levels, and ways to monitor students' progress. Together, team and department goals can improve school-home relationships, students' performance, the quality of instruction, and communication between teachers and students. The end result should be progress and increased achievement among all students.

Guiding the Process

Developing productive team and department goals results from a process that honors and includes all members. Knowing when to let go of your control of faculty and staff when it's in the best interest of these groups and of students will ultimately make you a more effective and respected principal. Although you let go, it's crucial to attend as an observer or a participant as many of these meetings as possible and to have the final one-page plans sent to you. There is a difference between being in control and being informed. You must be informed so you know what's happening in your school and can speak about these initiatives to the central office, to students, to parents, to the community, and to the media. Moreover, if a plan strikes you as being unproductive, you'll want to meet with the group and pose questions that move the members back on track before they try to implement the goals. For example, my Science Department came up with goals that were overly zealous; they included note taking, reading strategy lessons, writing to learn, hands-on experiments, and write-ups. My question to the group was, *Which of these goals do you believe is important for the upcoming year?* This helped the department decide on note taking and writing to learn. The teachers recognized that all their goals were top-notch, but their adjustments reflected the reality of being able to accomplish goals in a school year. In upcoming years, the science department would be able to include the other goals.

Continue to Think About . . .

As a principal, especially a new principal, you never can be too ready. My experiences and observations of other administrators have let me know that staff members are unforgiving when the principal is unprepared. Well-organized schools do not come about by accident; neither do well-organized classrooms. Both require a leader to plan ahead with purpose and to pay attention to details—a leader who listens carefully to staff and promotes improvements in students' achievement by asking faculty to set goals that respond to students' needs. School-wide improvement will move forward smoothly as long as you support these goals and the groups of teachers who create them.

Finally, reflect upon the questions below. Think about them as you continually reevaluate the full faculty and administrative meetings you run as well as the support team and/or department meetings that can improve teaching and learning.

- How did my first week with staff go? Did I make notes to myself of what worked well and what needs adjusting?
- Did my first faculty meeting accomplish the goals I set for myself? What went well? What can be improved? Did I write down my personal evaluation of the meeting?
- Am I communicating how I want to run my meetings? How am I leading by example? What do I need to do better?
- What meetings occur regularly in my school? Have I communicated how department and team goals can be a part of meetings? Do I need to form any committees?
- Does our faculty have a theme for the year? What am I doing to move this theme forward to contribute to the professional growth of staff?

Chapter 4

The Principal's Role in Evaluation and Mentorship:
Supporting New Teachers and Improving Instruction and Learning

• • •

It takes courage to release the familiar,
to embrace the new. In change there is power.

*- Alan Cohen, quoted in **Chicken Soup for the Soul***
by Jack Canfield and Mark Victor Hansen

It was my first year as a principal. With one more week until school opened, I arrived at my office at 7 a.m. to review my district's evaluation handbook. Reading the handbook was daunting. How was I going to manage this? There were forms for everything and strict timelines to meet. There were three evaluations for all teaching staff, and I had 65 staff members. Doing some quick mental math, I realized that I would be doing 195 evaluations! Besides evaluations, our district had an endless stream of forms for principals to complete: forms for pre-conferences and pre- and post-evaluation forms. All the forms needed to be signed, copied, and turned into the central office on specific dates.

When would I find the time to get it all done? How did my staff view the process? For me, it was more than quickly getting the meetings, observations, and paperwork done; I knew that if teachers didn't see the value in the process, they might view it as a waste of time. I also can recall asking myself if the school had a process for teachers to create goals or growth targets through self-evaluation. An even more pressing issue was that I had a lot of new teachers coming in and no existing mentor program. How could I get that program started?

As I look back on that day, I'm relieved that in my present position at Johnson Williams Middle School, I no longer have that evaluation system on my shoulders. A system that so comprehensive can push the administrator to find easy ways out. I've experienced this from both the teacher's and administrator's perspective. When I was a teacher, my administrator was so busy that he never evaluated me. He would call me in at the end of the year, give me the forms to sign, pat me on the back, and say, "Good work this year." At the time, I found it insulting, but now I can understand how evaluation demands pushed him to that point.

Good evaluation systems can foster communication and help teachers grow. Is there a balance point where teachers see the benefits and the processes are manageable? Finding that balance is a challenge, but I can assure you that doing so will make the year easier for all involved. When an administrator faces a large number of evaluations, it's important to manage time well. The only way I could complete 195 evaluations that first year was to set bimonthly goals concerning the number of teachers to evaluate. Even then, it was challenging because other things invariably popped up and disrupted my plans.

August and September are the time to start learning your district's evaluation system and to see what you can add to the process. The central office will let you know if you're to receive training in the system or if you're expected to learn it on your own. This can be a good time to have conversations with your staff about what they like about the present evaluation system and what areas they believe can be improved. As I've stressed before, these conversations send a message that you value teachers' input and recognize that all systems can be improved through feedback.

To gather feedback from teachers and staff, ask them the following questions.

- How were evaluations done in the past?
- Were the evaluations scheduled or unannounced?
- Is there an expectation for you as principal to do evaluations in a way that is consistent with your predecessor's?
- Did assistant principals evaluate teachers? If so, what kind of training did they receive to become competent evaluators?

Responses to these questions will vary, but the information will allow you to do a better job of fine-tuning and adjusting the evaluation process.

The Three Initiatives That Lead to Teacher Growth

In this chapter, I focus on three initiatives that an administrator can use to assist with and encourage teacher growth. These initiatives, listed below, move beyond those traditional evaluation standards and forms. To provide a broad management view, I have divided each initiative into three parts: what it looks like at the beginning of the year, the middle of the year, and the end of the year.

- Teacher self-evaluation and goal setting that places the responsibility of improving and learning on teachers themselves
- A mentor program that pairs experienced teachers with teachers new to your school and helps them adjust to your school's culture
- Class walk-throughs for you, your assistants, and master teachers that provide teachers with quick and meaningful feedback

1: Teacher Self-Evaluation and Goal Setting

• • •

Goal setting is stressed throughout this book because it is an integral part of my belief system. Goal setting for teachers is most likely already a part of your process; if not, it should be added. Encourage teachers to set goals for their own professional and personal growth. As I discussed in Chapter 3, they can use the SMART structure to create a plan for themselves as the year begins. (See p. 72.) Remember that it's up to you as the principal to keep the faculty focused on their goals for personal and professional growth. In this section, you'll explore the process that has worked for me.

I've worked in schools where reflecting on one's own goals is new to teachers and in schools where the process needs adjustments. Teachers usually bring up questions such as the following: *Will I be accountable for my goals? Will goals be part of my evaluation? Who do I share my goals with?*

To move the goal-setting process forward, I make it clear that the goals are personal and that the journey toward a goal is just as important as reaching it. Most important, I separate the goals that a teacher sets from the evaluation process.

September: Teacher Self-Evaluations and Goals

During the first two weeks of school, I meet with teams to discuss the idea of personal goal setting based on a self-evaluation model. I make it clear that I want written goals so they can be reread and adjusted throughout the year. I also tell teachers, *The goals you set will never be part of the formal evaluation process. These goals will not be placed in your files unless you choose to have them placed there.*

To add focus and clarity to the goal-setting process, I explain that at the end of the year the following two activities will occur; one is optional, the other is not.

- Teachers can schedule a meeting with me to discuss the goals they set, including their successes and challenges, or they can summarize their goals and achievements and turn these in to me for review.

- Teachers have the option of writing a reflection about their goals. I place this in their files only with their permission.

Self-Assessment Work Sheet

Carefully reflect on your teaching performance in all four domains. Complete the work sheet by circling your level of performance. Prepare to discuss your performance in all domains during the goal-setting meeting. Then choose one to three goals you wish to accomplish this year, and write them on a separate sheet of paper.

KEY: **U**-unsatisfactory   **B**-basic   **P**-proficient   **D**-distinguished

Domain 1: Designing Knowledge Work

1a.	Demonstrating knowledge of content and pedagogy	U B P D
1b.	Demonstrating knowledge of students	U B P D
1c.	Selecting instructional goals	U B P D
1d.	Demonstrating knowledge of resources	U B P D
1e.	Designing coherent instruction	U B P D
1f.	Assessing student learning through student-generated work	U B P D
1g.	Collecting, organizing, and analyzing data	U B P D

Domain 2: Organizing the Environment and Analyzing Data

2a.	Creating an environment of respect and rapport	U B P D
2b.	Establishing a culture that supports our mission	U B P D
2c.	Managing classroom procedures	U B P D
2d.	Managing student behavior	U B P D
2e.	Managing physical space	U B P D

Domain 3: Facilitating Knowledge Work

3a.	Communicating clearly and accurately	U B P D
3b.	Using questioning and discussion techniques	U B P D
3c.	Engaging students/time on task	U B P D
3d.	Recognizing student performance	U B P D
3e.	Differentiating instruction	U B P D

Domain 4: Professional and Leadership Responsibilities

4a.	Reflecting on teaching	U B P D
4b.	Maintaining accurate records	U B P D
4c.	Communicating with families	U B P D
4d.	Contributing leadership to the school and division	U B P D
4e.	Growing and developing professionally	U B P D
4f.	Showing professionalism	U B P D

(adapted from *The Three-Minute Classroom Walk-Through* by Carolyn J. Downey, Betty E. Steffy, Fenwick W. English, Larry E. Frase, & William K. Poston, Thousand Oaks, CA: Corwin Press, 2004)

Stating these end-of-year activities up front lets everyone know that I'll be following up. Of course, it also puts me in the position of making sure that I do follow up!

Next I pass out my self-assessment work sheet (see p. 85) and encourage teachers to use it to help them think about their professional work. The form has four categories, but teachers can step out of the form and create other meaningful goals. Often teachers ask if they have to write a goal for each area. The answer is no. The form's purpose is to encourage reflection so teachers set goals that are meaningful to them. This may mean one goal or five goals; the choice is theirs.

My challenge to teachers is simple: Complete the form within a week. Create goals that are meaningful—goals that will add focus to your professional and personal life. Since this is a self-directed activity, I have little control over whether the goals transform a staff member. The process encourages teachers to reflect on what they do, and hopefully, it motivates them to improve and progress. The philosophy behind teacher goal setting and self-evaluation is that the best change is change that we choose to make and to achieve for ourselves. Choice is empowering and motivating.

What follows are some examples of teacher-created goals. Note that they range from professional study to supporting students' families.

● This year I will attend our state middle school association conference, gather information for other departments, and hold an after-school debriefing for interested faculty members.

● I will read Robert Marzano's research on instructional strategies and work to incorporate them into my classroom practices by the second semester.

● I will become a member of our local Phi Delta Kappa Chapter and attend all the meetings this year. In addition, I will share what I learn with my team.

● I will conduct two home visits to families of students by November 1.

January: Teacher Self-Evaluations and Goals

The goals written in September can grow dormant if you don't refocus teachers on them in January. At my first faculty meeting of the new year, I like to remind teachers of the process they went through in September and the value of continually revisiting their goals. I start by asking the faculty to reflect on a simple question: *How many of you can recall the goals you set for yourself, and are you aware of your progress?*

As a transition, I share some of my goals and honestly let teachers know my progress. (See Appendix K, p. 179). Honestly, I've never had a year when I could say that I was on target to meet all my goals. Even if I was, I probably wouldn't say so, for I understand that most teachers won't be in that situation.

Leadership Tip:
Making the Meetings Run Smoothly

After a few minutes of nonschool conversation, I turn the teacher's attention to his or her goals by posing one or more of the following questions:

● Tell me about the goals you created for yourself this year.

● Which goals did you achieve? How did you achieve them? Is any goal still a work in progress? If so, how do you plan to bring it to completion?

● How has this process helped you grow as a professional?

● How could you move this process into your classroom? Would the process work with your students? How would you manage it?

I always close the meeting by asking questions that invite the teacher to tell me how I can better support her and the process of goal setting.

● What could I have done better to motivate the staff to achieve their goals?

● Did I remind you enough or too much about your goals?

When the meeting ends, I give the teacher positive feedback and ask if there's anything I can do to assist with any unmet goals. I again remind the teacher that she has the option to write down her goals and progress toward them and I will place that summary in her personnel file. This action allows teachers to have a choice, which is empowering. Some teachers ask me, "What will happen if I don't decide to write down my goals?" I always make it clear that nothing will happen. The choice is theirs, and I respect it.

Then I tell the faculty that I'll be including goal-accomplishment reminders in my weekly staff e-mails, and that at the end of the year each teacher and I will have a personal conversation about the goals they set and their path toward achievement. I add that at the end of the year they'll have the option to summarize their goals and progress and may have the summaries added to their files—and I always stress option.

Late May to Early June: Teacher Self-Evaluations and Goals

The end of the year is an opportunity for you to bring the teacher goal-setting initiative to completion and demonstrate your ability to follow through. In September and again in January, I made it clear that self-reflection would be part of a conversation at the end of the year and told teachers to build in time for reflection and for a meeting with me.

About four weeks before the end of the year, announce to teachers that you'll be setting up the goal-reflection meetings. This announcement can be made at a faculty meeting or through e-mail. Teachers who meet with you should have their goals written down and expect to engage in a conversation about their efforts to achieve their goals. If there are any goals they haven't met, they should be able to explain why and whether they will place those unmet goals on next year's list.

If your faculty is small—around 30 to 35 teachers—you can start this process three weeks before the school year ends. I suggest that you schedule a maximum of three to four 15- to 20-minute meetings a day, as the end of the year is hectic. Don't overextend yourself. I've found that I need a 20-minute break between meetings to tend to other matters that always arise. If you can't accommodate all the meeting requests, use the week after school closes to complete the process. If necessary, you can meet with five to six teachers per day then.

If you have a large staff, you won't be able to meet with every teacher. In that case,

ask teachers who wish to talk about their goals to e-mail you to set up a meeting. Those who don't want a face-to-face meeting can give you their self-evaluation forms and summaries of their progress and their reflection about their goals, if they choose to write one; they will also need to let you know whether they want these placed in their files.

2: Establishing a Peer Mentoring Program

● ● ●

I can still recall the sound of her sobbing and deep breaths today. This was during my third year as a sixth-grade reading-writing teacher, and I was packing my briefcase before heading home. I heard a tentative knock on my closed classroom door. When I opened it, the new Spanish teacher walked in. "Can I talk to you?" she asked. As I nodded, she broke down. Her sobs grew louder each moment. In a few minutes, but what felt like an eternity to me, she managed to explain that she felt overwhelmed and was doing everything wrong. "I don't remember all the stuff we heard at the first faculty meeting," she said. "I didn't turn in my attendance. I didn't know I should collect lunch money. I want to leave now!"

You can replay this scenario in schools throughout the country—schools that don't provide continuous support for new teachers. Assuming that new staff "knows the ropes" is not a platform for teacher success or for reducing turnover. Unfortunately, teacher turnover is a reality of our profession, and reducing it should be our goal. A mentor program is one piece of the puzzle for maintaining a stable faculty.

What Makes a Good Mentor?

Part of the program's success is seeking out good mentors. This should not be done by assignment; you'll be more successful if you offer it by invitation. Exceptional mentors are veteran teachers who are good listeners, empathetic, flexible, and positive. They manage time well, are skilled classroom managers and instructors, maintain confidentiality, offer choices to their students, and have positive relationships with students and peers.

Try to pair new staff with veterans who will be a good match. Pairing a quiet new staff member with an extremely extroverted veteran may not work; as one new teacher told me, "I never had a chance to say much or ask questions. He meant well, but I needed to talk, too."

In addition to encouraging your teachers to set professional goals, it's also important to initiate a yearlong program that supports inexperienced teachers and experienced teachers who are new to your school. A mentor program pairs an experienced and new teacher. Over the course of the year, the teachers meet several times a month to review tasks that need to be completed and to anticipate upcoming responsibilities. Putting a mentor program in place ensures that all new teachers will be able to successfully handle tasks that veteran teachers complete automatically—tasks such as collecting and delivering attendance and lunch money, and where and when to turn in interim reports and report cards.

STARTING AN EFFECTIVE PEER MENTOR PROGRAM

Before school starts, you can quickly connect new teachers to veterans, have the veterans run through school procedures, and let all the staff know that mentors will see new teachers if concerns arise. This model is not a formalized program, however, and it most likely won't give new staff the support they need to feel successful in and adjusted to the school.

A formalized mentor program requires that you set up meetings with clear agendas as well as create a monthly calendar of issues that the new and veteran teacher should discuss. I've found that the following four elements provide the basic framework for a peer mentoring program:

- Connect a new teacher with a veteran teacher for the year.
- Help new teachers understand the ins and outs of every school procedure.
- Make sure the schedule has multiple opportunities for new teachers to dialogue about victories and challenges.
- Provide new staff with support for planning lessons, tips for managing a class, effective behavior and discipline guidelines, an understanding of the school's grading policies, recess and lunch duties, and so on.

At my school, I've established one mentor meeting per week for the first month, followed by two meetings per month for the remainder of the year or as needed. Meet with your mentors to share the following list of their responsibilities, and encourage discussion among the group:

- For the first month of school, meet with your new teacher at least once a week.
- Remind new staff that it takes time to learn the culture; patience is a key to progress.
- Do not overload new staff with information; move slowly so they won't feel overwhelmed.
- Review discipline policies, class management, grading, interim grades and reports, report cards, attendance, use of e-mail, and whom to seek out if they have a question.
- Be a good listener so you can find out where new staff might need support.
- Maintain a confidential relationship.
- Assist the new teacher with Back to School Night, and explain what to expect at parent conferences.
- Share tips on how you manage tasks such as planning, dealing with angry parents, and how you handle time effectively during a day.

When mentor teachers know the expectations about their role, you can set up a meeting with them and their new teachers. This meeting is an opportunity for you to review expectations, be positive about the year, connect new staff with their mentors, and frame a meeting schedule for the first month of school and beyond.

MAKING TIME FOR A MENTORING PROGRAM

A mentoring program won't work unless you set aside time for the new and veteran teachers to meet during the school day. Meetings can take place during a common planning time or during part of a scheduled faculty meeting, or you and an assistant can cover the class of the veteran or new teacher (or hire subs) so both classes are covered. I find that pairs will meet on their own, too, but if teachers are to feel that mentoring is important to you, then you need to reserve time for the program during the school day.

Topics of the mentor meetings can vary according to your needs. Below is a yearlong calendar I developed at Warren County Junior High School in Front Royal, Virginia, with key topics that I've updated from *Redefining Staff Development* by Laura Robb (2000a). You can add areas that relate specifically to your school and delete issues that don't. I recommend that you review and update this peer-mentoring calendar annually. The most effective way is to ask the mentors and new teachers to do this at the end of the school year. Then you and your assistants can review their recommendations and tweak the calendar.

Calendar for Peer-Mentoring Program

Key: **PP** = peer partner   **NT** = new teacher

Initial and date each item on the line at the left after you complete it. Some items are repeated because they occur repeatedly during the year.

Suggested Timeline for August

___ Welcome your NT partner with a telephone call. Introduce yourself, explain your role, and provide information about the school's culture and the community.

___ Schedule a tour of the school building, highlighting important places: mailboxes, classrooms, faculty room, nurse's and guidance offices, location of media equipment, teachers' parking lot, and so on.

___ Introduce important personnel: secretaries; department heads; guidance counselors; librarians; and music, physical education, art, special education, and reading teachers.

___ Provide the following assistance with school procedures:

___ Secure and review curriculum guides and textbooks.

___ Review the process for completing and turning in beginning-of-school paperwork.

___ Review opening day.

___ Review the items in the teacher handbook: fire drill, plan books, sign-in and sign-out sheets, ID badges, leave policy.

___ Discuss all schedules that affect the NT.

___ Discuss attendance procedures.

___ Discuss arranging for a substitute.

___ Discuss required classroom rules and management systems.

___ Help NT arrange classroom and plan for the first day and week.

___ Share management strategies that work for you: how to set up a grade book, keeping track of homework and tardiness, using administrators to help.

___ Review curriculum guides and discuss upcoming topics.

___ Review due dates for interim reports and marking period report cards. Have NT post these behind or on his or her desk.

___ Review your school's way for students to head their papers and journals.

Suggested Timeline for September

___ Negotiate meeting and interaction times with NT.

___ Share your plan book and ask NT if she or he has questions.

___ Check on how NT is doing with grading and assessment.

___ Show NT how to set up students' work files.

___ Help NT prioritize workload.

___ Plan and assist with Back to School Night.

___ Share ideas on how to interact successfully with parents.

___ Model telephone calls to parents that give positive feedback on their child.

___ Review curriculum guides and discuss upcoming topics.

___ Review leave procedures and engaging a substitute.

___ Review field trip policies and procedures.

___ Discuss professional study opportunities.

___ Discuss religious holiday policies.

___ Show NT locations of students' cumulative folders and health files and how to use them.

___ Compliment NT on his or her enthusiasm, follow-through, and so on.

Suggested Timeline for October-December

___ Negotiate meeting and interaction times with NT.

___ Provide NT with assistance during the first interim and grading period: comments, grading system, computerized grading.

___ Review snow-day policies and schedule changes.

___ Assist NT in planning first parent conferences.

___ Review grading system and any special forms to be completed.

___ Review referral process for child study and special education.

___ Encourage NT to observe other teachers, including you. Ask administrators to arrange to cover NT's class.

___ Celebrate positives NT shares; write a note or send an e-mail that praises NT's progress.

___ Be sympathetic to NT's concerns and arrange for additional support from administrators if necessary.

___ Visit NT's classroom as a support, not as an evaluator.

___ Review curriculum guides and discuss upcoming topics.

___ Explain picture day and how this affects teaching schedules.

Suggested Timeline for January-February

___ Negotiate meeting and interaction times with NT.

___ Review policies and issues regarding retention and failure of students.

___ Discuss exam policies and share old exams with NT.

___ Review end-of-semester grading policies and procedures.

___ Review curriculum guides and discuss upcoming topics.

___ Prepare NT for midyear conference with principal.

___ Let NT know of all the progress he or she has made in an e-mail, a note, or a conversation.

Suggested Timeline for March-June

___ Negotiate meeting and interaction times with NT.

___ Review curriculum guides and discuss upcoming topics.

___ Share suggestions for maintaining students' interest at the end of the year.

___ Share how you reduce end-of-the-year stress levels.

___ Review the following policies:

    ___ updating students' literacy profiles and cumulative folders

    ___ completing retention procedures if necessary

    ___ completing final grade reports

    ___ following "closing the year" procedures

___ Take the time to celebrate all the first-year successes in a note or e-mail.

August-September: The Principal's Role in the Mentoring Program

Most meetings will occur between the mentor and new teacher, although you can attend a few. I urge you to let pairs discuss issues freely on their own, for your presence can inhibit questions and reactions. Moreover, these meetings are a perfect opportunity to let a teacher develop leadership. Just be sure pairs are ready for the task ahead and show your support of the program through conversations and e-mails, and by setting aside time for pairs to meet during the school day.

During the group meeting of mentors and new teachers that occurs near the end of August, I give out the calendar. Ask teachers to read it, and field any questions. Review the number of meetings to be held through December and the time you have set aside during school for these meetings. Explain that pairs can meet as often as they need to and that meetings can be a few minutes or up to an hour, depending on what they need to discuss. Inform the group that you'll hold another meeting in January and at the end of May or early June.

January Check-Up: The Principal's Role in the Mentoring Program

January is an excellent time of year to take stock of your mentor program. I hold two group meetings: one with mentor teachers and a second one with mentors and new teachers.

Meeting with mentors gives you the opportunity to find out from their perspective how new teachers are adjusting to the school. Generate conversation by having each mentor come to the meeting with ideas that have worked for them as well as suggestions for making the process better. Mentors will enjoy learning tips from other veterans who have made the process work well. Also, the meeting should include discussions of things that went wrong and how to avoid repeating such mistakes.

Bringing mentors and new teachers together in January gives you the opportunity to encourage discussions about positive interactions between pairs and to adjust future meeting schedules. It's important that you be informed of any changes to regularly scheduled meetings. Explain to pairs that the veteran teacher will have more input on the frequency of meetings, as veterans know what to expect in the upcoming months. And although the mentors and new teachers have calendars, I always suggest that a mentor cover the topics below with a new teacher in January. (These are suggestions, not requirements.)

- Review the grading systems.
- Offer class management tips. What is working? What needs improvement?
- Do a peer observation with the goal of helping the new teacher. Negotiate a focus for the observation. For example, the observation can focus on a new teacher's mini-lesson, guided practice, organization of group work, or class management.
- Find ways to celebrate the positives, and send a note to the new teacher with specific praise.
- Discuss how to deal with midyear stress and/or winter doldrums.

This midyear meeting is also an opportunity to collect feedback on the first half of the year from the new teachers. This is an ideal time for questions and answers and an opportunity to reflect on the year and what lies ahead. I like to e-mail the questions below to new teachers about two weeks prior to our meeting so they can mull them over. These questions can help to improve the process.

- How has our mentor program helped you transition to our school?
- What aspects of this program do you recommend we keep?
- What are some things that we did not prepare you for?

  What could we have done better?
- Do you feel support from your mentor?

  What does your mentor do to make the adjustment to our school easier?

Some suggested changes, such as the number of upcoming meetings or class observations, can be implemented in the last months of school. Others, such as carving out additional time for the mentor program and items to add for August and September meetings, are placed on the discussion agenda for the following school year.

Late May–Early June: The Principal's Role in the Mentoring Program

Hopefully by this time, your new teachers understand the daily workings and expectations of your school and have had a successful first year. Wrap up the year by having an informal meeting of mentors and new teachers. I prefer a casual and collegial atmosphere over lunch. You might meet with two or three groups at a time; this depends on the number of teachers new to your school. Even though the meeting is informal, I do keep the following questions in my mind to ask:

- As you look back on your first year, how did this group and having a mentor help you?
- New teachers will arrive in August. What can we do differently next year to make their adjustment to our school's culture easier?

These questions send a key message to teachers: I value your feedback. I am committed to your success and will use the constructive comments you provide to improve the first year for our future new teachers. In addition, this debriefing allows me to honor and praise new teachers' first-year efforts and their successes in the classroom and as colleagues. Notice, too, that this debriefing is what a good teacher does in his classroom with students.

As a principal, I always want to demonstrate my commitment to learning from others, to their successes, and to be open to collecting feedback on ways to improve.

3: Use Class Walk-Throughs for Visibility, Support, and Feedback

When I was a first-year teacher, my administrator told our faculty, "I want to be more visible in classrooms this year." I can recall chatting about this with my colleagues and thinking it was a good idea. One day, the principal came to my class, stood in the back for five minutes, smiled, and left the room. Yes, he was more visible, but since I received no feedback, I felt that the visit was of no benefit to me. And I yearned for feedback and suggestions for improving my instruction to students in reading and writing.

How can you use class visits to increase your visibility and to provide feedback to teachers? A class walk-through program can be part of the answer. Teachers value feedback from administrators that can improve instruction. Organizing a walk-through program can provide them with immediate suggestions that can improve their teaching and student learning.

August-September: Class Walk-Throughs

August and September are thinking and planning months. To create an effective classroom visit program, you'll need to design a regular schedule in August for visiting classes and providing feedback. No doubt, you'll revisit the schedule in September and the months that follow to make adjustments. If you're a new principal, you can organize your walk-throughs by department or grade-level teams. Veteran principals will want to consider conducting walk-throughs in the classes of teachers with whom they worked in the previous year on improving instruction and discipline as well as in new teachers' classes.

In a large school you can send an e-mail to all teachers on a grade-level team or in a department letting them know that you'll be conducting walk-throughs for the next two weeks. In a small school, you can send this e-mail to grade levels or announce it at a faculty meeting. Each class visit should be 10 to 20 minutes, depending on the purpose of the visit. For example, if I want to observe how a teacher organizes time at the start of class, then 10 minutes is enough. If my goal is to observe a mini-lesson, group work, or teacher-student conferences, my visit will be 15 to 20 minutes.

WALK-THROUGHS:
COLLABORATION BETWEEN YOU AND TEACHERS

In my first position as principal, I set a personal goal of observing instruction and teacher interactions with students in three to five classes per day via walk-throughs. On most days, however, five walk-throughs was an unrealistic goal. One to three short walk-throughs was all I could manage. With longer time frames, one a day (two at the most) worked best for me. In addition, I wanted to provide teachers with genuine feedback that celebrated what was working and offer one or two suggestions that would spark reflection and growth.

Since immediate feedback is the overarching goal of walk-throughs, the teachers and I collaborated to develop a feedback form. (Feel free to develop your own.) I prefer forms that have checklists and a place to write some comments so I can celebrate what I observed, and/or pose a question that starts a teacher thinking about change. The completed form should be placed in the teacher's box the day you complete the walk-through.

During my second year as principal of Warren County Junior High, a quick classroom visit program that I wanted to implement became a test of my communication skills. I met with teams and explained my goals. Then came my mistake: I created a feedback form on my own. Three weeks into the program, an eighth-grade teacher approached me. She appeared tentative and nervous, but she blurted out, "I was hoping for more feedback than a short note."

My response was candid, and as I look back, I realize that it helped to save the program. I told the teacher that I was struggling with offering feedback because I didn't have any guidelines. When I asked if she had any suggestions, she broke into a relieved smile. She had an excellent suggestion: Develop a checklist with an area for additional comments and then give the form to faculty and collect their feedback. Always make sure you honor your faculty's input by including some of their suggestions. Walk-throughs affect your teachers in positive and sometimes in negative ways. I believe that teachers should have input in evaluation policies that affect their teaching.

The next day I had the draft of a form that included a checklist, and I asked the teacher to collect feedback from each team about the checklist and the entire form. We ended up with subject-specific checklists that addressed all teachers' concerns, including reading and writing strategies, questioning techniques, and the amount of teacher talk compared with the time reserved for students' independent practice. (See Appendix L, pp. 180–181.)

Additionally, my staff requested that I frame any concerns as questions or using word choice that shows sensitivity to teachers' feelings. For example, I might write: *Do you think students need more time to respond?* or *I noticed how well you supported a group of struggling learners, but try to remember to give specific guidelines to those not working with you.*

Instead of bristling and becoming defensive when the teacher approached me about feedback, I replied in a way that showed I genuinely cared about teachers' needs and valued their feedback. Confrontations with teachers relating to walk-throughs can be minimized if you first think about the do's and don'ts of this effective method of observing faculty.

THE DO'S OF PRODUCTIVE WALK-THROUGHS

You and your faculty can create effective walk-through forms that highlight what your school considers effective teaching; therefore, forms will differ among schools and should have differences among some subject areas. For example, a science form in my school includes items addressing hands-on experiments and inquiry learning. In Spanish, the form includes teaching language through conversation.

It will take about two weeks to develop forms that meet the needs of your school. The following suggestions can help you with this process:

- Do meet with the entire faculty and explain the purpose of walk-throughs and how these can support their teaching and students' learning.
- Do make sure teachers understand that walk-throughs mean they'll be seeing more of you and your assistants in their classrooms.
- Do explain to teachers that you want to see teaching occur in a natural context frequently. Your presence shouldn't be a disruption to the class; the more you visit classrooms, the less your presence will be noticed.
- Do organize a committee of volunteers to work with you on framing drafts of walk-through forms for the entire faculty to review and edit. I find it helpful to show old versions of the walk-through forms to committee members as a starting point. This makes their job of framing new forms easier. They understand of what kind of feedback the forms should elicit.

Leadership Tip:
Procedures and Tips for Successful Walk-Throughs

When I first started doing class walk-throughs, I found myself losing track of which teachers I had visited and when. To avoid missing any classes or repeatedly visiting the same class, try the following suggestions:

- Keep a list of teachers and the periods they teach.

- Create a sheet that has each teacher's name. Leave space to record the date and time of your visit. This list or log will become your memory bank.

- Visit classrooms and use the walk-through form to record information. Be sure to fill out a few positives on the sheet, especially if you need to point out a specific concern to the teacher.

- Jot down any areas of need you notice. You'll review these in January, do a second walk-through, and then meet with the teacher to discuss your observations only if you don't observe progress.

- After completing the form, fold it, and place it in the teacher's box. This assures that several important goals of a walk-through are met: feedback is immediate; there is a purpose for your visit; and you are demonstrating that you follow through.

- Review your walk-through logs in January and February.

- Evaluate the process in June.

- Do give drafts to faculty to review at a meeting. Doing this at a meeting helps busy teachers. I find that using faculty time means I receive feedback from everyone, and that's my goal.
- Do review teacher input with your committee and create a form that incorporates teachers' needs. (See Appendix L, pp. 180–181 for blank walk-through forms and examples of completed ones.)
- In August and September, do create a walk-through schedule through the end of the calendar year. You can create a schedule for the second half of the year over your winter break or in early January. Aim for one to two walk-throughs a day.

THE DON'TS OF PRODUCTIVE WALK-THROUGHS

- Don't use a form that you found on the Internet that worked for another school. It may not meet the needs of your school.
- Don't make creating the form a top-down decision. I build consensus for the same reason I conduct walk-throughs: it's an effective way to support teachers and students.
- Don't use walk-throughs to point out negatives instead of building on what's working.

If you can be consistent with walk-throughs during the first three months of school, your teachers will become accustomed to seeing you more in the classroom. Equally important, you will have established a way to support instruction and students' learning.

January or February: Class Walk-Throughs

First, reread your log of visits to determine whether you've been consistently making one, and when time permits, two walk-throughs each day. Your goal for this time of year is to have visited each classroom at least twice. Of course, this depends on the size of your school. In an extremely large school, you might conduct one walk-through and your assistants conduct the second.

As you review your log, keep the following questions in mind: *Which areas show positive results? Are there any areas of concern? If so, what am I doing about them? Do my visits spotlight areas of instruction or class management that staff development could improve?*

For example, as I reviewed my logbook one year in January, I noticed that some teachers needed assistance with generating effective warm-up activities that open a class and focus students on a specific subject, while many teachers did an excellent job with these activities. To address this issue, I asked a teacher who was proficient with this strategy to offer two after-school sessions on how to start a class with an effective warm-up. Attendance was optional for many teachers, but I had several teachers who I felt really needed to be there, so I set up individual meetings with them to negotiate their attendance at one of the two sessions. I was up-front and made it clear that a week after the sessions, I would do a walk-through at the start of their classes to see if their warm-up activities had improved.

I like to rely on my in-house experts to provide staff development and growth opportunities for the rest of the faculty. There is no cost to the school, it provides leadership opportunities for teachers, and it allows our programs to be tweaked immediately.

Late May or Early June: Class Walk-Throughs

If you've been diligent with this program, teachers will be seeing you as a more visible principal, one who gets into classrooms daily and provides supportive feedback. The end of the year is the ideal time to reflect on your visits and on how walk-throughs can be improved next year. Take a look at your classroom visit log to see how many visits you made during the year.

Listed below are questions I ponder and jot down answers to—I find that writing helps me clarify my feelings and observations and pinpoint ways to improve things. If you don't write your responses as you self-evaluate, you might forget the perspective you had at the time. Moreover, you can revisit your answers in August when you're gearing up for a new school year and use them to move forward and improve walk-throughs.

- Did I effectively manage this initiative? How can I improve my management of this process? What went well? What aspects do I want to keep in place for next year?
- As I reflect on my visits, what are the strengths of our staff? What are several areas that need to be improved? Can I improve walk-throughs on my own? Do I need to find additional staff development opportunities?

If time allows, I also like to seek feedback from teachers to bring the collaborative process full circle. The end of the year is a good time to do this. Create a short survey of three or so questions. Teachers won't want to complete a long survey at the end of the year. Give a deadline date for the survey to be returned. Or have teachers complete the surveys at a final faculty meeting to ensure that you receive responses from everyone. My experience is that the number of responses and their quality will increase if the survey questions are limited. Here are some sample questions.

● Did our form allow me to provide you with helpful feedback? Give an example.
● What aspects of the form could be improved? Please give a specific example.
● Was I more visible in your classroom this year? Does that make a difference to you? If so, how?

This feedback, along with your personal reflection, will help to improve the walk-through process for the upcoming school year. If you find that walk-throughs have been a success, then it's time to expand the model to your assistants and to teachers.

TWO WAYS TO EXPAND WALK-THROUGHS

One way to expand this initiative is by training your assistants to do walk-throughs. As part of the training process, I complete several walk-throughs with my assistants. This is easy to do and can be beneficial for their growth and mine. For these walk-throughs, I contact at least three teachers to let them know that an assistant and I will be doing walk-throughs in their classes; it's important to notify teachers as this shows respect and consideration.

My assistant and I complete the walk-through and fill out separate forms. Then we debrief and compare notes to see if we saw the class in a similar way. If we noted different concerns, we discuss options for addressing them. When both of us feel confident, I let my assistant conduct walk-throughs without me. Assistants log their visits just as I do. I believe that as principal part of my job is to help train my assistants to be future principals. Walk-throughs are a way to help assistants be seen in a leadership role and at the same time improve their knowledge of instruction and classroom management.

Another way to expand walk-throughs is by inviting master teachers to assume a leadership role and learn how to complete walk-throughs. Master teachers come from the ranks of classroom teachers, department chairs, or team leaders. I extend invitations because I believe teachers should have a choice and feel comfortable conducting walk-throughs. The ideal time to make this move is in January or February—if walk-throughs are going smoothly and productively. If they're not, wait until another year.

Having teachers complete walk-throughs transforms the model into peer observation. A word of caution: Make it clear that these are teacher-to-teacher observations, and that you, as administrator, need to be out of the loop. The effort will fail if faculty believe or perceive that these teachers are reporting everything they see directly to you. If the model works well, teachers will have an opportunity to see colleagues teach, learn from what they see, dialogue, and note areas that they believe can be improved. I find that when teachers observe areas of need, they request staff development or opportunities to observe in other schools for their team or department.

Walk-throughs permit you to provide positive feedback and support to teachers all year long. There are times, however, when you'll observe a teacher engaging in inappropriate behavior or instruction that's below the level you find acceptable. It's important to be honest with a teacher and then offer as much support as possible to help the teacher improve. Unfortunately, there will be times when you'll have to document your conversations and requests in order to protect yourself, other teachers, and students.

DOCUMENTING TEACHERS:
A PAINFUL YET NECESSARY PROCEDURE

Your school district may have a written policy and guidelines for documenting staff issues. If so, become familiar with or review this document during the summer. If a staff member has done something inappropriate, such as cursing at a student during class or making threatening comments to a parent during a conference, you may feel the only option you have is to document the incident. The following four guidelines for documenting an employee's actions and possibly sending a disciplinary letter come from my experiences and conversations with other principals:

- Make a note of the date and time of the incident.

- Write a detailed and objective summary of the incident and file it. At this point, you may only choose to keep a written record and not send a formal letter to an employee.

- Note a specific course of action for the employee, both in the short- and long-term. Documentation may lead to a formal letter being placed in the employee's file or the development of a plan of improvement. Review the guidelines for this step in your school district's policy.

- If you write a letter of reprimand, place a copy in the employee's file and a copy in your confidential file. Often, an employee will write a rebuttal; place copies in both files as well.

Letters to employees should be your last resort, not necessarily your first choice. In cases when you've met with and counseled the teacher several times but the problem arises again—for example, using inappropriate language in the classroom again—sending a formal letter with a plan of improvement may be necessary. However, remember that letters and plans of improvement, which may place a teacher on a year's probation, can build anger and frustration and result in an adversarial relationship between the two of you. Moreover, this negative energy can rub off on other staff members.

Once, a history teacher in my school resigned in August, and I had to hire a replacement quickly. Late hires can put you in a weak position, for many of the most qualified teachers already have positions. The alternative of opening the year with a string of substitute teachers was discouraged by the central office, so I hired Richard to teach history.

After two weeks, students' complaints about Richard were streaming into my office, followed by telephone calls from parents. Both groups requested transfers to other history sections. To verify these complaints, I observed several of Richard's classes. There was no basic organization in his classroom: he didn't take attendance, the room was messy, and students were completing stacks of work sheets instead of participating in hands-on learning experiences. I found myself having to squelch anger at the people who had made excellent recommendations on Richard's behalf.

Immediately, I assigned a peer coach to Richard, set up weekly meetings with him so I could help him plan lessons, and told him that I would do at least two entire class observa-

tions a week so we could dialogue about instruction and organization. For two weeks, I observed some progress. Then Richard started missing meetings with his peer coach and with me. Parent and student complaints continued to escalate. That's when I made the decision to move to more formal documentation.

A letter and a face-to-face meeting with Richard expressing my concerns about his teaching brought about no change. Next I wrote a plan of improvement that outlined Richard's responsibilities toward his team, required him to meet with his peer coach and with me, and outlined the times we would meet to work on his lesson plans and discuss ways to deal with students' behavior. Additionally, the plan informed Richard that I would make several unannounced observations of his classroom each week. Richard's behavior remained unchanged. Moreover, teachers complained that he wasn't attending team meetings and he frequently left his students unattended to drink a soda or a cup of coffee. At this point, I arranged a meeting with our district's director of personnel. We both agreed that offering Richard the option of resigning now or being fired was the best course of action; he chose resignation. We also agreed that I would look for a long-term substitute teacher or a permanent teacher to replace him. So I advertised the position, taught Richard's classes for four weeks, and found a solid candidate who is still teaching at the school today.

Fortunately, such situations don't occur often. The huge number of complaints from parents, teachers, custodial help, and students made the choice to let Richard go in the middle of the year easier. Not addressing such an extreme situation can reflect poorly on you. It sends the message that you tolerate poor teaching as well as irresponsible behavior. Dealing with tough situations is part of the principal's job.

Continue to Think About . . .

This chapter focused on three initiatives you can start in your school this year: teacher goals and self-evaluation, a peer-mentoring program, and class walk-throughs. The message embedded in the initiatives is inclusiveness. That message generates motivation among faculty to make each initiative succeed and a broader desire to improve instruction and student learning and to close the achievement gap.

I realize that some readers will have these programs in place already, while others will have some or none. Either way, I encourage you to consider whether these programs can be added to your school or whether you can make your existing programs better. Use the questions that follow to evaluate these initiatives and how to involve staff as a way to strengthen them.

- Am I collaborating with teachers and administrators when designing, implementing, and adjusting initiatives?
- Do I send e-mails to staff reminding them of the goal-setting process and what their next steps should be?
- Do I take enough time to build consensus among staff members for initiatives that affect their daily lives at school?
- Do I provide teachers with timely and positive feedback after completing walk-throughs and longer observations?
- Am I delegating some of the responsibilities for walk-throughs to my assistants? To master teachers?

Chapter 5

The Principal as Instructional Leader:

Closing the Achievement Gap

With Initiatives That Work

● ● ●

The role of the leader is to ensure that the organization develops relationships that help produce desirable results.

- Michael Fullan

As I've mentioned before, my first year as a principal was in Warren County Junior High School, in Front Royal, Virginia. The school was new, which meant I spent the summer prior to the opening day monitoring the final phases of construction; hiring faculty and secretaries; working with available teachers to order furniture, blackboards, tables, chairs, bulletin boards, band instruments, library bookcases and tables, gym equipment, office furniture, and computers; and helping design a telephone system with a local company. I had carefully tucked instruction into the back of my mind, but I didn't actively consider what my role as instructional leader would be until the end of August.

My faculty was a mixture of teachers who were new to Warren County and teachers who had transferred from the local middle and high schools. My personal goal for this new school was to help teachers develop best-practice instruction that would support every student's achievement and progress. With more than 800 eighth and ninth graders arriving in the last week in August, this was a tall order. The school didn't have a literacy coach, reading resource teacher, or staff developer, so my first thoughts were that I had to do it all. It didn't take me long to abandon that idea, especially after I contacted several principals in Warren County and nearby counties to discuss this issue.

My conversations and experiences with other principals and faculty that year and in the years that followed enabled me to develop a definition of instructional leadership that works for me: *As instructional leader, my job is to not do it all but to find ways to make it all happen.* This means that I enlist support from my assistants, teachers, and parents; delegate responsibilities; and ensure that others keep me informed. It also means that my assistants and I attend as many of the meetings and programs dedicated to improving instruction as possible, read all the professional books and articles that our faculty studies, attend conferences, and keep abreast of research in education.

Improving teaching, which in turn improves students' achievement, can be accomplished as long as you build consensus for professional learning among teachers. Remember, too many projects geared to improve instruction in one year can cause overload and frustration among everyone, and not being able to follow up can have more negative effects than starting small. Since I've covered professional study and sharing among faculty at team and full faculty meetings, as well as faculty book studies, in Chapter 3, I'll focus on the following six ideas in this chapter:

1. Promoting professional development includes finding the funds for bringing in educators for inspiration and for ongoing study.

2. Collecting data on students' academic performance and behavior problems is crucial to knowing as much as possible about both areas, and can support instructional planning and the development of a support program.

3. Building instructional consistencies at your school, including the development of school-wide plans for areas of learning such as common proofreading marks, classroom rules, and opening class warm-up activities, raises the comfort level of students as they travel from class to class and maintains a common language that makes learning more accessible.

4. Nine-week assessments serve as a diagnostic tool for teachers, who can use the data to inform their instruction and plan interventions for small groups or individuals.

5. Ongoing weekly performance-based assessments enable teachers to evaluate students' progress and immediately plan beneficial lessons and interventions.

6. Moving to best-practice instructional strategies for all requires continual teacher training and benefits students' learning and achievement.

The premise of this chapter is that the principal must guide, coach, and champion instructional initiatives while balancing the demands of the job. No school can be highly effective if there is only one instructional leader. For a school to flourish, the environment must encourage all staff to seek out leadership opportunities that are congruent with the mission of the school; and for this to occur, the following three things need to be in place:

● The principal needs to assess honestly his strengths and weaknesses in order to know what he can do well and what he should delegate to others.

● Staff must be actively involved in professional development in order to be responsive to and meet the ever-changing needs of students.

● Teachers and administrators must interact with key instructional leaders. These leaders can be master teachers, department chairs, or resource educators hired to work with faculty and administration.

Your Instructional Leadership Impacts Teachers and Students

Expanding your instructional leadership from your areas of expertise to the entire building can be a daunting task. Most of us feel confident in the area in which we taught and continually ask ourselves, *How can I be knowledgeable in all subjects?* The key is to work with your teacher leaders and allow them to lead with you. Principals who do this can foster their professional growth in different subjects and develop leadership among faculty.

As principal, one part of your job is to move initiatives forward, even though there is sure to be some resistance to change among the faculty. Change is challenging. Some teachers resist change because of previous experiences or the fear of leaving their comfort and control zones. Working staff through those issues is a fundamental challenge of effective leadership. I like to meet with teams or departments to discuss new initiatives, hear their concerns, and build support for the initiatives among them. Doing this can bring most teachers on board; not doing it can derail your project. Avoid pushing too hard or moving forward with an initiative without your teachers' backing and understanding. When you push too hard or move too fast, people shut down or more actively resist. Reserving time to plant seeds of understanding and to build consensus before plunging into a new instructional initiative develops the commitment among faculty that can create effective change.

It's important to understand that resistance will always be present; an effective principal, however, accepts this and moves on with the job by continually working with resisters to build support. In my opinion, those who choose to continually harmonize or placate staff will never become effective instructional leaders because they avoid making any positive change.

The reflection statements below sit on my desk. I reread them frequently because my responses to them change depending on where my teachers and I are with instructional initiatives. I encourage you to use these statements to support your instructional leadership.

- I do not do justice to this job if I compromise my convictions for personal gain or popularity.
- I need to constantly grow and hone my personal belief system and increase my professional knowledge.

- If I can honestly say that my decisions are in the best interest of children and my staff, I feel comfortable.
- I need to continue to develop my sense of purpose, interpersonal skills, self-awareness, empathy, emotional self-control, humility, and unwavering commitment to my students and faculty.
- My actions and words represent our school.
- My efforts at work should be for others, not myself.

As you revisit these statements, it's also important to consider the research on leadership and to extract points that can form the foundation of your instructional leadership style. An effective principal is like a master juggler: he has to keep key programs that support teachers and students all in motion, without dropping any of them.

WHAT RESEARCH SAYS ABOUT LEADERSHIP BEHAVIORS

Instructional leadership is only one piece of the puzzle for the effective school principal. Leadership combined with trust is the glue that binds everything together. Even if you fully understand many of the skills of leadership, you also must understand that building trust takes time and that it's the key to positive principal-faculty interactions.

For instructional leadership to flourish, certain key behaviors need to emanate from the principal's office. Sheppard (1996) synthesized the research on instructional leadership behaviors. He confirmed that there is a strong relationship between instructional leadership behaviors by principals and teacher commitment, professional involvement, and innovation. According to Sheppard, there are eight key behaviors connected to the professional growth and performance of administrators. The behaviors are listed below, along with queries to help you reflect on each one.

1. **Forming and communicating school goals:** *Does the principal effectively articulate and define school goals?*

2. **Supervising and evaluating instruction:** *What role does the principal have in the supervision and evaluation process? Is the principal actively involved?*

3. **Coordinating curriculum:** *Are efforts made to better redefine, pace, and organize the curriculum?*

4. **Monitoring student progress:** *What systems are in place to monitor how students are learning? What intervals are established to get instructional feedback? Is the information effectively used?*

5. **Protecting instructional time:** *Is instructional time seen by staff as a priority? Does the principal communicate a belief that instructional time is a priority?*

6. **Maintaining high visibility:** *Is the principal seen by teachers in the hall and, more importantly, in the classroom? Is classroom observation feedback provided to the teacher on a timely basis?*

7. **Providing teacher incentives:** *Is the principal motivating and rewarding staff to continuously improve?*

8. **Promoting professional development:** *Is the principal seeking out professional development that is meaningful to staff and revisited throughout the year?*

On paper, the eight behaviors may seem simple, but living by them is a challenge. If you practice and develop these instructional leadership behaviors, your faculty is more likely to view you as their school's instructional leader. What I hope you find interesting is that the behaviors are "macro," rather than a list of particular instructional skills or teaching strategies.

Sheppard's research points out two behaviors that principals must exhibit—behaviors that have the most impact on the school community: forming and communicating goals and promoting professional development. The more teachers engage in goal setting and professional study, the more effective they become, because they continually revisit, refine, and revise their theory of how children learn and use these revisions to improve students' learning.

1: Promoting Professional Development and Efficacy

Efficacy is a teacher's personal belief that he can make a difference in the lives of children. Foundational efficacy, efficacy that grows and lasts, needs more than the enthusiasm of new, young teachers. Efficacy that can impact teaching and students' learning develops when teachers study professional literature, attend conferences, share ideas, take graduate classes, and work with other professionals in the field.

In my experience, new teachers tend to have a high sense of personal efficacy; they come into the job wholeheartedly convinced that they can do the job and make a difference. More often than not, I've seen these new teachers fizzle out, usually by the winter holiday.

There can be many reasons, but one I've repeatedly observed is that new teachers have a limited repertoire of instructional strategies; they tend to have a few that they use daily whether these work or not. When students don't get it right away, new teachers feel it's either their fault or the students'. As a result, these teachers begin to lose their personal efficacy. If strong staff development is in place and teachers are learning and practicing research-tested ways to present material, they can better support children's learning. As novice and veteran teachers alike experience success by learning and using new instructional strategies, they gain more confidence and continue to develop their theory of how children learn. To me, one of the key roles of a principal is helping faculty recognize that they'll benefit from participating in professional study and learning new ways to teach.

FINDING WAYS TO BRING A VARIETY OF PROFESSIONAL STUDY INITIATIVES TO YOUR SCHOOL

Ongoing professional study using the resources within your school—book studies, conversations about professional articles, and lessons that teachers share during team, department, and full faculty meetings—are initiatives that you can and should put in place immediately. Once you organize this type of professional learning, you can have teachers and your assistants maintain the momentum. (See Chapter 4, pp. 81–108.)

It's also advantageous to bring in experts from outside your school and district and to build a large professional library of books and journals for all subjects. Accomplishing this takes money—money that schools don't have. In the sections below, I'll explain how I funded each professional study initiative at my school. (Even though I only strive to break even, in many cases my school actually makes money! The extra funds go into an account to pay for the next year's programs.)

Outside Experts: During my first year at Warren County Junior High School, I surveyed teachers to discover their professional study needs. More than 90 percent of them wondered if the school could hire an outside expert to lead part of their professional study. With a limited staff development budget, my initial feeling was that I couldn't meet their request. But I wanted to support my teachers, so I brainstormed lists of ideas—and one worked!

Our area has several universities that are from 15 to 45 minutes away from the junior high school. I wrote letters to the department of education of three universities to invite a

Leadership Tip:
Learning Beyond the School

In addition to bringing experts into your school, it's beneficial to encourage teachers to learn beyond the school. Have them observe colleagues at their own school and teachers at other schools. Support this by helping teachers find schools to visit and by hiring substitute teachers to cover their classes. I also encourage you to use extra funds to send teachers to state and national conferences. Not only is getting away enjoyable, but also your teachers will learn a great deal and have much to share.

new professor to consider doing professional development at our school at a reduced rate. The benefit to the professor would be to hone his workshop skills. One professor, John Fahey, responded, and for two years, he worked with different departments. My teachers were able to study with an expert who also had a great deal of middle and high school teaching experience.

Inspirational Speakers: Although they only come for one or two visits, inspirational speakers can do a great deal to spark the motors of an initiative, get teachers on board, and get the initiative moving forward. I'm able to bring in speakers like Ruth Culham and Laura Robb each year by opening up the day to other school districts in the state. Ruth Culham has reviewed the use of the six traits for assessment and planning instruction, and Laura Robb has shown teachers how to use diverse texts to differentiate reading instruction.

About six months before such a workshop, my assistant principal and I develop a brochure that advertises the workshop and includes costs. We e-mail them to assistant superintendents and principals in Virginia several times. The workshop has now become an annual event. Financial support from the other school districts provides the funds to bring in these speakers and allows us to give each attendee a copy of the speaker's book.

A Professional Library for Teachers: A professional library provides teachers of all subjects with access to the finest journals and books. Our school funds professional books and journals by hosting an annual Scholastic Book Fair. The points earned from the fair can be used to purchase professional and trade books. This frees my librarian to use part of his budget to purchase professional journals and magazines that support all subjects.

Your instructional leadership can guide teachers toward understanding the value of professional development and working together as a team to improve student learning. Knowing how to collect data on students' achievement and behavior and how to use this data to improve instruction and students' learning is an important part of professional development for all teams and departments.

2: Collecting Data to Improve Teaching and Learning

• • •

"Show me the data" is a statement I frequently make. I want proof that things are or are not working for a student—and not only proof from standardized testing, but also proof that emerges from performance-based or formative assessments. In this section, I'll review three data collection categories that can improve students' performance and teachers' instruction:

● Data collection and students' performance at school
● Data collection on school discipline
● Data collection and your guidance department

By collecting and tracking this data, you, your assistants, and teachers can adjust and scaffold instruction for students who need assistance and pinpoint students who can bene-fit from challenges. Before you ask teachers to collect data about students, discuss the fol-lowing questions with your assistants:

● What key pieces of data do you presently track?
● What measures outside of testing data do you and your faculty use to monitor the effectiveness of instruction?
● How are your teachers presently involved in collecting data?

Once you have fleshed out these questions and have a clearer picture of the level of your school's data collection of student performance and behavior, discuss the questions that follow with teachers at a full faculty, team, or department meeting:

- Which areas of students' school life need to be studied more closely to improve their learning and achievement?
- What can we learn about our students and ourselves from this data?
- How can the data we collect help improve instruction and student performance?
- How many people do you think need to work together to collect data?
- What can the administration and front office do to support data collection?

You should set up two to three meetings so teachers can discuss the issues and arrive at suggestions appropriate for your school and population. When you invite teachers into the planning process for collecting data, they can see the advantages of doing some additional work and investing in their professional improvement and in their students' development and performance.

Compiling data is the first step. Analysis is the second step. For the data to be useful, groups need to interpret what the information means and then plan instructional interventions that can help teachers support their students' learning. The list below contains suggestions gathered from several faculty conversations at Johnson Williams Middle School in Berryville, Virginia, where I am presently principal. (The list you compile may have similarities but also differences because of your location and the population you serve.)

For each data-collection area, I've included what the information can tell teachers and administrators as well as some possible interventions. Creating effective interventions is the heart and soul of the process, and as teachers and administrators collaborate to interpret data, they come to see the need for positive change.

DATA COLLECTION ON STUDENT PERFORMANCE
- Number of students on honor roll
- Percentage of students in advanced classes
- Number of students involved in after-school clubs
- Number of students involved in athletics per season
- Grades of students participating in extracurricular activities
- Number and names of students failing one or more subjects
- Number of library books checked out each month

What Data on Student Performance Can Tell You About Instruction

You can gain insight into whether

- the academic program challenges students;
- the academic program meets the needs of diverse reading levels;
- library circulation needs to increase;
- there is a correlation between students' grades and their involvement in extracurricular activities; and
- instruction and good intervention plans are in place.

Possible Instructional Interventions

- If the student failure data is an issue, you and the administrative team can study the data to generate questions and ideas such as the following: Are certain teachers failing a high number of students? Is more professional development needed?
- Consider more work on differentiating instruction or the use of new research-tested instructional strategies. You might also think about whether the school needs to take a deeper look at interventions that can prevent failure.
- Work with your athletic director of after-school sponsor to create a plan to involve more students in after-school programs.
- Have your librarian work with language arts teachers to organize a school-wide reading program with the goal of getting more students in the library and encouraging them to check out books they can and want to read.

DATA COLLECTION ON SCHOOL DISCIPLINARY ACTIONS

- Number of in-school suspensions by grade level and gender
- Number of out-of-school suspensions by grade level and gender
- Number of bus referrals and bus suspensions by grade level and gender
- Number of referrals sent to the office each month by gender, including the teacher's name and grade level

What Data on Student Disciplinary Actions Can Tell You About Instruction

You can gain insights into whether

- instruction is engaging, for discipline referrals tend to go down when all students learn;
- office referrals are coming predominately from just a few staff members or, less likely, are coming equally from all staff members;
- a class environment is positive, with active student learning;
- a teacher is firm but fair and has created trust between students and him; and
- struggling students can participate in and make productive contributions to this class.

Possible Instructional Interventions

- Initiate a conversation between you and a teacher who has a high number of disciplinary referrals to explore why this is happening.
- Set aside time to do two to four consecutive observations in the teacher's problem classes. Behavior problems are usually related to teaching style. Students who can't read the material, who struggle with listening to and taking notes during a 30-minute lecture, and who lack the background knowledge and vocabulary to comprehend the topic frequently misbehave to show their discomfort.

- Pair a teacher who needs to improve instruction with a master teacher. Encourage the teacher to observe the master teacher and continue the meetings.

- Complete follow-up observations that point out progress and offer more suggestions for improvement.

- Provide staff development programs on lesson planning, best-practice instruction, and classroom management.

- Meet regularly with teachers and ask them to assess their progress and express any ways you can support them.

DATA COLLECTION FROM THE GUIDANCE DEPARTMENT: What It Can Tell You About Instruction

- Number of students referred to the guidance office per month
- Number of child study requests (if this is the domain of guidance)
- Monthly student attendance

What Data From the Guidance Department Can Tell You About Instruction

You can gain insights into whether

- teachers or teams of teachers can resolve student issues;
- teachers are consciously or unconsciously labeling a student instead of finding ways to help that student succeed; and
- poor attendance records are affecting academic performance.

Possible Instructional Interventions

- Work with a guidance counselor, and meet with faculty to review the referral process to guidance. Include the interventions a teacher or team should try before sending a student to guidance or recommending a student for child study.

- Study how each team utilizes guidance, and open a dialogue with teams that are sending student after student to guidance.

- Work with the guidance department and parents to discover the reason for large numbers of absences from school and try to improve the student's attendance. Imagine how effective your school could be if you developed and interpreted a list of similar indicators, kept good records, and ultimately used this data to chart your school's progress. However, the responsibility for managing data collection and study can't be carried by one person alone. The goal is to get all teachers and assistants involved in the effort. Spread out areas of responsibility, and establish timelines for collection.

MAKING DATA COLLECTION WORK

A data-collection initiative requires the principal to be fully invested in the task. This means speaking about its value frequently, repeating the message in e-mails, and gently nudging staff to turn in the required data.

When I started the initiative, I gave certain areas of responsibility to my assistants. For example, one administrator took guidance data as his area. The other took on discipline referrals. They met with the counselors and assisted in coming up with ideas for how to collect and manage the data and established timelines for when the data needed to be turned in to them. After the administrators received the data, they reviewed it and then sent it to me. At first, I reminded teachers and administrators several times per month to keep up with their areas of data responsibility. Over time, I reminded them less and less, and eventually not at all. Teachers and administrators knew I expected data from them at the end of

Leadership Tip: Making Data Collection Work

For any organization to run effectively, the leader must be able to count on others. My assistants began to see the value in their pieces of data and became committed to the end-of-the-month deadlines I set. Soon, instead of my leading the effort, my assistants and I were leading it. The same pattern happened over time with others who were responsible for key pieces of data. I managed the process tightly at first, but I slowly let go when I saw real commitment to the program.

the month, and they turned it in. This is an excellent example of keeping tight reins on staff and then gradually releasing responsibility to them.

The challenge for all principals is to cultivate a mind-set among staff that says, *We value data and understand that interpreting it can support continuous instructional improvement.* The following three suggestions can support you in this endeavor:

Suggestion 1: Putting the Data Collection Effort Into Motion

The first step is to decide the areas for which you want to collect data. The list on pages 118–122 describes the pieces of data that my school collects. Again, you can use the list as a guide and adjust it according to the needs of your school. For instance, in my school, the academic performance of student athletes has always been important. Therefore, it makes sense to have a system in place to track who our athletes are and how they do academically. Your goals may be similar. Focus on what your school needs. The list of the three categories that my faculty, assistants, and I created is large and can be intimidating at first, but when you break it down into smaller areas (with staff members responsible for their areas only), it becomes doable.

Establish deadlines for when data needs to be turned in to you. Some will be monthly, such as data for student discipline, library circulation, and parent contacts. Other deadlines, such as for seasonal athletic participation and honor roll data, are on different schedules.

Suggestion 2: Using the Data to Set Goals

It's critical for the principal to have a method of organizing the data and communicating the results to faculty and assistants. I store all data on my computer and send monthly summaries to the entire staff through e-mail and hand them out in our professional study faculty meetings.

Remember that this program takes time to reach full effectiveness; it will work best for your school over the long term. After a year of collecting key pieces of data, you can set monthly goals for the coming year and begin comparing the current year's data to previous year's. Sometimes the goal is to bring about an increase, and sometimes it's to bring about a decrease. For example, our school library book circulation goal might be to increase circulation each month by 10 to 15 percent. This links to instruction because a wider library use indicates that students are spending more time practicing reading and doing research and other projects. On the other hand, a goal for discipline might be to decrease in-school suspensions. I meet with teachers and my assistants at the end of the year to have conversations about the data-conversations that challenge them to set a higher or lower monthly goal for the next year.

Seeing the data moves us to a conversation of what we need to do to improve. For a library, it might be for the librarian to sponsor a school-wide reading program. Such a program can increase library circulation and the number of books and magazines that students read. In another case, our in-school suspension data recently showed that most suspensions occurred in one grade level and a very high percentage of suspended students were boys. The discussion with my assistants and team leaders centered around the following queries: *What does this pattern mean, and why is it occurring? Were referrals mostly from a few teachers or were they spread out? What can we do better to help our boys in that grade level increase responsibility and engagement? Do we need to form a committee to explore different ways to run our discipline program? Finally, what is a reasonable monthly decrease goal for next year?*

Without a doubt, discipline affects the learning of the disruptive students as well as that of the entire class. After collaborating, teachers devised the following plan of action:

● Talk one-on-one to disruptive students and find out what's behind their behavior.
● Scaffold instruction and offer extra help after class for students that are struggling.
● Find alternative texts on a topic that students can read.
● Pair up students so partners can help each other and make the learning process more social and less intimidating.
● Examine assignments and class work and try strategies that are more hands-on for students.

What teachers discovered was that 90 percent of the students who received in-school suspensions couldn't read the textbook. Behavior issues and referrals decreased over the next several months, as teachers provided tutoring, found other texts, permitted students to work in pairs to select important details and discover big ideas, and set up an after-school homework support program. Without data collection, the issue might never have surfaced, and behavior problems would have continued.

Suggestion 3: Creating a Data Board

You can involve students in reaching data goals by posting several key pieces of data on a bulletin board in a prominent area of your school. I suggest posting items such as the following:

- Number of library books checked out each month by grade level
- Number of students on honor roll by grade level
- Number of students participating in athletics and clubs by grade level
- Student attendance rate each month by grade level
- Number of students involved in clubs by grade level
- Number of students participating in athletics by grade level

Posted items should be positive and should never single out anyone. I like to announce the data at the beginning of the month and to challenge our student body to have higher numbers the next month, and I only post data in areas that students can support. Decreasing suspensions, behavior referrals, and failing grades are the responsibility of teachers and administrators.

With the board in a prominent place, students gather around it during lunch, when they change classes, and when they arrive in the morning to see how their school is using goals and data to make improvements. Many teachers in my school use similar data-tracking boards in their classrooms. They chart data such as number of books read or percentage of students completing their homework. This information can be used to motivate students to improve, and at the same time, it invites them to be part of the data gathering initiative!

Additionally, I have found that this type of data contains information that my superintendent wants to see. You can send data to your superintendent or a central office director each month, depending on the size of your system. (See Appendix M, pp. 182–186, for an example of a monthly data summary.) If you commit to sending data, be consistent and get it in on schedule. Missing deadlines with your central office is a poor reflection on you. Meeting deadlines shows that you're serious about collecting data and using it to improve instruction, students' learning, and overall school performance.

All schools have formal and informal power structures. The principal and assistants occupy the formal seats; often, respected veteran teachers occupy the informal seats. An effective administrator will be aware of which teachers have the respect of their peers and will work on building a positive professional relationship them. Frequently, their support will be needed to launch a new initiative.

Data collection is an excellent way to deepen your knowledge of the instructional needs in your school by pinpointing key areas and monitoring them. Along with collecting data to improve instruction, it's also beneficial to develop a productive learning community by identifying instructional consistencies that can involve all teachers without compromising their teaching styles.

3: The Benefits of Building-Wide Instructional Consistencies

March 1999 was an important date for me; I was offered my first principal's job, which included opening a new school. Opening a school is a challenge, but with that challenge came the opportunity to set some new initiatives in place over and above the soft initiatives that always can work. I wanted to take advantage of that. When the staff and a school is new no one can say, "This is how we've always done it." Andrew Keller, my associate principal, and I had dozens of conversations to focus us on the kind of culture we hoped to develop and then to hire staff that shared our beliefs.

A large number of the new hires would be inexperienced teachers who would need support. Moreover, with seven periods a day, students would have seven different teachers with diverse teaching styles and different ways of organizing class routines. That is not necessarily negative, but it can pose challenges for some students.

Andrew and I tossed around ideas for peer evaluation, a mentor program, and how to help all the staff organize instruction for student success. Our conversations centered on how we could provide students with consistent routines and class organization. We wanted a school that honored and celebrated creativity among teachers, but we also wanted students to experience comfort through consistent class routines. We took a chance and developed what became known in our school as "building-wide consistencies."

Both of us worried that veteran teachers who came from other Warren County schools might resent the program. So before moving forward, we met with experienced teachers to explain the program and begin a dialogue about it. We candidly told them that we wanted their support, and we encouraged open discussion. All of the veteran teachers applauded and joined the effort. With them on board, we knew the program would succeed because they promised to communicate with and mentor new and inexperienced teachers.

BUILDING-WIDE CONSISTENCIES DEVELOP A PRODUCTIVE LEARNING COMMUNITY

At Warren County Junior High School, building-wide consistencies included eight strategies that teachers agreed to make part of their daily routine. These strategies are used throughout the school in every subject area. Faculty quickly became committed to making building-wide consistencies a part of their daily routine with students because they understood that the consistencies could buy them more instructional time and create a positive structure for students. Review the consistencies that worked for my teachers and ask yourself if they could support students and their learning at your school.

Eight Building-Wide Consistencies

1. Greet students at your classroom door: With this simple act, the teacher sets a tone of caring and respect for students and also sets a positive tone for each class period. In addition, when teachers stand outside their classrooms, they're visible and become an important part of managing students' behavior and safety.

2. Open class with a warm-up activity: At the beginning of each class, the teacher provides a brief warm-up activity to focus students on the content of the class. The activities should relate to the day's instruction or review important concepts. As the state testing date looms, warm-up activities can focus on curriculum review and test-taking skills. Such activities should take no more than four to seven minutes of class time and should be written on the chalkboard or an overhead transparency. After students are greeted by the teacher, they complete the warm-up while the teacher checks roll. Such activities quickly focus students on their new class and save valuable class time.

3. List daily learning objectives: Each day, after students complete their warm-up activity, teachers should quickly review the objectives and relevant state standards for that class. My teachers have agreed to post these learning objectives on the same area of the blackboard, where they can be referred to quickly by teachers and students as class unfolds. This consistency maintains the academic focus.

4. Post daily homework assignments: Teachers always write the daily homework assignment on the same place on the chalkboard so students can easily locate it and copy it in their notebooks. It's also important to reserve enough time at the end of class for students to record these assignments. Homework should be used to reinforce concepts and ideas presented in the classroom and should not count for more than 20 percent of a student's grade for that class.

Keep in mind that homework is part of the overall grading issue, which is a huge topic. I've worked in schools where homework counted as much as 75 percent and as little as 0 percent. In some schools, teachers give three to five grades per week, and in other schools, they give three to five grades per grading period. This is unfair; it shouldn't happen, but it does. Setting a maximum percentage for homework will help avoid this discrepancy.

5. Post classroom rules: Teachers should post their classroom rules on a wall or bulletin board that students can easily see. Rules should be created and negotiated with the students. Always state rules using positive language—what students *should do*. Remember, rules established by students and teachers should enable a class to run smoothly and students to respect one another and their teacher. Class rules are expectations, not punishments. When students help write class rules, they learn responsibility and build a stronger class and school community. Periodically, the teacher should set aside a few minutes to review class rules. With repeated review, the rules remain in the forefront of students' minds.

6. Develop and use a standard format for written assignments: The English Department in my school created a standard format for written work that was approved by all the teachers. A format provides consistency and direction for all written assignments. The format that our school uses is simple: On the upper-right-hand side of the paper, students write their full name, subject, assignment, and date. Teachers encourage the use of pencils or blue or black ink. In each class, teachers keep a canister of pencils and pens in case students arrive without them, so learning remains the focus of each class.

7. Use common proofreading marks: This practice provides students with consistent correction marks on papers in all classes. The English Department in my school developed these and taught them to other staff.

8. Provide a meaningful wrap-up activity: Teachers close their classes by recapping the important topics covered and by communicating several positive learning behaviors they observed such as pairs working productively, excellent questions raised, or full participation. We encourage teachers to dismiss classes creatively by using vocabulary and question-answer reviews rather than by relying on the bell.

These building-wide consistencies are not new to teachers. My hunch is that most effective teachers use some or all of them on a daily basis. The key to their effectiveness is that the entire faculty makes a commitment to incorporating them into their daily routines.

This type of program is more challenging to implement in a well-established school. It can be done, but it will take some time. As principal, you should first determine how much consistency is already in place in your school. I suggest that you begin in the area where you have the most consistency and try to spread that specific consistency to all subjects. Then set aside time to discuss the benefits of the one or two school-wide consistencies to stimulate discussion on adding more.

A building-wide consistency program is easier to implement if the school is either new, low performing, or has a high percentage of new staff (more than 30 percent). Such schools recognize the need for improvement, and faculty are more willing to move forward with new but well-documented initiatives.

THE BENEFITS OF BUILDING-WIDE CONSISTENCIES: STUDENTS HEAR AND SEE THE SAME MESSAGE

Whether a student is in a health or a history class, the basic framework is the same: the teacher greets her at the door, she participates in a warm-up activity with her classmates, learning goals and the homework assignment are written on the board, and so on. The less time students spend adjusting to how individual teachers structure their classes, the more time they can spend learning. Moreover, building-wide consistencies make the transition to the school easier for new students. An eighth grader entering Warren County Junior High pointed out to me, "When I walk into a classroom, I know it will start with a warm-up. It's great to know where to find the homework assignment and goals and know how the class will end."

Not only do the consistencies support students, they also generate conversations among teachers—conversations that ultimately improve instruction.

TEACHERS USE BUILDING-WIDE CONSISTENCIES TO INCREASE COMMUNICATION

On any given day, as staff members stand in the hall near their classrooms or eat lunch in the faculty room, I hear them speaking to each other about how a particular warm-up activity worked or about successful ways to wrap up a class. It pleases me when teachers share strategies because it shows their level of commitment to students' learning. In many cases, such conversations led teachers to ask me or my assistants to cover one of their classes so they could observe colleagues using a specific warm-up or wrap-up activity. The conversations eventually led to reading strategies and writing techniques, and teachers gathered the support and feedback from colleagues that ultimately could improve instruction.

Communication among teachers can spread to department meetings, where they have the time to discuss issues such as how to best create warm-up activities or use warm-ups to review key curricula objectives. During my second year as principal of Warren County Junior High, I attended an English department meeting and observed the group unanimously vote to use the building-wide consistencies as part of their self-evaluation process. When English teachers chatted about this decision with their colleagues, the history and science departments decided to use the consistencies for self-evaluation, too. Talk can be positive and stimulate beneficial changes, especially when talk surrounds an initiative that's working smoothly.

HOW BUILDING-WIDE CONSISTENCIES AFFECT TEACHERS AND STUDENTS

When teachers embrace a program such as building-wide consistencies, it increases their pride in their school, and it becomes a guidepost for hiring new teachers. By explaining our school's way of doing things during an interview, Andrew and I were able to hire teachers who would support the school-wide initiatives. Moreover, with building wide consistencies, we never heard statements such as *You're taking away from my creativity* or *I can't teach using a structure.* We believed that the structure of building-wide consistencies would allow teachers to be more creative instructionally because they gained extra teaching time. How people teach is an individual thing. As principal, I may pose questions, arrange professional study workshops for growth, or suggest a book, but I don't demand a specific teaching style. Teacher feedback indicated that because the consistencies gave them more instructional time, they were able to better use and enjoy their individual teaching styles.

This program created consistent routines for students in every class, making both the transition to the school and moving to the next grade level within the school easier. Part of

Leadership Tip: A Feedback Framework

You can develop a chart with your building-wide consistencies and use it to complete quick observations. When you visit a class, check off the consistencies on the chart, provide positive feedback, and possibly suggest an area that needs adjustment. Then place the completed chart in the teacher's box. Finally, make a notation of the date and time of the visit for your own records. This chart is an excellent tool for gathering data on any of the consistencies to study and improve them.

instructional leadership is ultimately orchestrating programs school wide, and building-wide consistencies allowed this to happen in my school. If you implement an assessment program as a building-wide consistency, your school can use in-house testing to measure students' progress and to plan instruction.

4: Nine-Week Assessments: A New Take on Traditional Exams

Most middle and high schools have traditional exams that cover a semester's worth of material and sometimes count as a large part of a student's grade. I can recall that when I was in high school I had anxiety before, during, and after exams; I'm sure this rings true with many people. I would take the test, usually do poorly, and the class would move on. No one seemed to worry that I hadn't mastered the material. In many classes, such as math, the new material builds on the old so, if a student does poorly on the first semester exam, he most likely will continue to do poorly for the remainder of the year. Nine-week assessments can replace traditional exams and support instruction because teachers analyze these assessments and use what they learn to plan instruction and meet individual student's needs. Nine-week assessments can replace traditional exams and support instruction because teachers analyze these assessments and use what they learn to plan instruction and meet individual student's needs.

In a time of standards, schools need to move toward diagnostic assessments. These are assessments that provide data about student progress and help a teacher reflect on the instructional adjustments needed to ensure that students are learning, improving, and moving forward. If the mission in education, and your school, is for all students to learn, then moving to nine-week diagnostic assessments is one way to support that mission. However, I encourage you to reflect on the four questions and answers that follow before plunging headlong into this type of assessment. In addition, you'll need to address teachers' reluctance to give up the final exam and their reluctance to cope with schedule changes. Other roadblocks to this change may include class schedules and limited teaching equipment and parental and community opposition.

Question 1: How do your teachers view exams? How enthusiastic are your teachers about exams?

Personally, no teacher has ever told me that they love exams. Exams can be frustrating: teachers have to write them, get them approved, and then stop teaching to review the material. Most teachers are happy to change to nine-week assessments, especially when they see how this kind of assessment can improve their teaching and students' learning.

Question 2: Do you feel your teachers are receptive to giving up exams?

Even if you sense that your teachers will embrace this change, I urge you to have open discussions with key instructional players such as literacy coaches, curriculum developers, and team leaders or department chairs. I never recommend making decisions based on presumptions. These conversations may take time, but they're an excellent opportunity to get a sense of your school's pulse.

Question 3: Is your curriculum aligned to state standards?

With the advent of state standards, many schools have worked to align their curriculum with them. Terms such as curriculum mapping, assessments, and pacing guides are now common across our country. The nine-week assessment initiative should only be implemented in subjects for which your school has mapped and aligned the curriculum. Otherwise, your assessments might not provide data that reflects students' knowledge of the state curriculum.

Question 4: What exactly are nine-week assessments?

Nine-week assessments are carefully developed diagnostic tests given at the same time by teachers who teach the same subject. Teachers collaborate to develop these 50-question assessments, which reflect the material that's been covered. They pay particular attention to test construction: the length of the test, the type of questions, and the relationship of each question to a specific state standard.

The nine-week assessment should have questions similar to those on your state test; this is critical, for it helps students become test-wise. It's also critical that you be aware of how your state constructs its test. For instance, in a Virginia school, a nine-week test that only contains knowledge-based, factual questions would produce predictive data that is insufficient because Virginia also tests students' inferential thinking. Yes, students may show mastery on knowledge-based questions, but how will they do if the same content is tested in a way that requires higher-level thinking? So the type of questions and their quality, as well as their ability to address state standards, are all important issues for you to consider.

To transform objections to nine-week assessments into support, it's important to understand that this shift from traditional final exams can inform and improve teachers' instructional plans by supporting the learning of all students, from those who struggle to those who do well. Knowing these benefits will enable you to respond to groups who oppose this change. In the section that follows, I've focused on how nine-week assessments help teachers plan lessons that meet and support diverse students' needs.

NINE-WEEK ASSESSMENTS ENCOURAGE TEACHER COLLABORATION AND INFORM INSTRUCTION

I have teachers administer the nine-week assessment three times during the year. Students take the third assessment three weeks before state testing; this is the benchmark assessment (Herman & Baker, 2005). Consistency is critical, which is why members of a department collaborate to construct their test and administer it to all their students. Moreover, all students receive the same study guide, also designed by department members, so they can review the same material prior to the nine-week assessment. Using a common study guide is a way to ensure that students review the same material at school. Reviewing material in class provides another constant, for assigning this as homework can result in some students studying more than others. Teachers in a subject decide on the number of review periods they will set aside, again, to ensure the consistency of the data.

The First Nine-Week Assessment Test: After students take the nine-week assessment test, teachers of the same subject collaborate to analyze the data. They're looking for students' strengths and weaknesses in terms of content. Teachers also look at which types of questions students had difficulty answering—inferential, cause and effect, factual, sequence, and so on. Additionally, they can look at their data based on AYP (Annual Yearly Progress) subgroups. This allows teachers to go back and refocus instruction on areas that are weak. The principal can use this data to ask questions and to challenge teachers to find creative ways to reteach those students who don't demonstrate recall and understanding of the content. Teachers can organize students who need support in pairs or small groups and help them review content or practice specific types of questions, while other students can work independently on reading and/or writing or problem solving in math. The data from the assessments are used to go back and reteach rather than to give a grade (Chappius, 2005).

The Second Nine-Week Assessment Test: The second nine-week assessment test differs from the first assessment in one aspect: it contains five to seven cumulative review questions based on material covered in the previous nine-week assessment. The teacher can assess recall and understanding of the second nine-week period, and also check students' retention of the key concepts and information included on the first nine-week test. Results of the second nine-week assessment test open the door for teacher-to-teacher conversations within a department so that they can refine the assessment tests, as well as seek ways to improve students' long-term recall and understanding of specific information. As principal, your responsibility is to work with staff to provide effective teaching support by offering appropriate professional articles to read and discuss and by inviting instructional experts into the school to work with teachers.

The Third Nine-Week Assessment Test: This test functions as a final benchmark assessment. It always includes review questions from the previous two assessments plus new material covered. This benchmark test should be given four weeks before students take the state-mandated test. Having a few weeks gives teachers time to analyze the data and use it to guide review for small groups or the entire class.

My teachers and I also use the data to predict student performance on the state test. Ultimately, if the correlation between the two is high, we probably have a good test. If not, the assessment and benchmarks may need adjusting for the next year.

TRANSFORMING ROADBLOCKS TO NINE-WEEK ASSESSMENTS INTO SUPPORT

Once you know the kinds of objections different groups in your school community will make about moving away from traditional exams, you can prepare some responses and engage them in conversations that enable them to see the benefits of changing to nine-week assessments. I don't want to make this seem easy—it's not. People cling to their past experiences and comfort zones. It took a school district next to mine three years of negotiating with various groups before final exams could be transformed into prescriptive assessments. A sure-fire way to remove roadblocks to change is for you and administrators to provide detailed information that can help groups change their belief systems.

Strong Areas	Areas of Need
• Department chairs are effective, enthusiastic educators. • Curriculum is aligned to state standards. • Teachers want to improve their instruction and close achievement gaps between students.	• Creating diagnostic tests with factual questions and questions that demand critical thinking was a skill that teachers needed to practice and hone. • Finding the time for staff to work on a common assessment test posed challenges. • Developing effective data-analysis skills among staff and interpreting the data required a large time commitment. Department chairs and teachers could complete this work on early release days and during common planning periods. • Recognizing that developing and interpreting tests would vary among departments, for some groups worked faster and more efficiently than others.

Roadblock 1: Class Schedules and Teaching Equipment. Each school has its own unique situation that may make it harder or easier for the principal to implement nine-week assessments. For example, I worked in a school that had multiple science classes with limited lab equipment. Labs couldn't be scheduled at the same time, which caused a problem with maintaining the curriculum so all science classes would be prepared for each nine-week assessment. Since the science department divided its curriculum into several units of study, I suggested that each teacher work on a different unit of study during the same period of time so each class would have access to lab equipment. Then science teachers collaborated to design nine-week assessments for each unit. They administered an assessment when they had completed a specific unit of study.

Roadblock 2: Parents and Community. When parents and community members say, *We've always done it this way,* they're telling administrators and teachers that they support exams and other traditional teaching methods such as lectures and detentions and suspensions because that's what they experienced and they want the same for their children. However, maintaining traditions is not a valid reason for continuing specific programs or teaching methods.

Since parents and community members tend to judge schools by their own personal experiences, the more you deviate from the traditional, the more you'll need to educate, inform, and involve parents in the process. Getting better at using assessments and analyzing data to guide instruction is a step in the right direction—and it's definitely a step that parents need to understand. My approach to educating parents includes scheduling three coffee meetings from 7:15 a.m. to 9:00 a.m. at which parents can meet with me and department chairs to air their concerns, ask questions, and hopefully come to see the wisdom of our decision to switch to nine-week assessments. If this isn't enough, then I continue scheduling open conversations. I also find it helpful to summarize the discussions that teachers and administrators are having regarding the initiative in school newsletters, on the school's Web site, and via e-mails. The more information that parents and community members have, the easier it will be to help them move away from traditional exams and their own personal school experiences.

NINE-WEEK ASSESSMENTS: MOVING THE INITIATIVE FORWARD

I can still recall the interview for my current job. One interviewer asked me a question about school-wide initiatives for data collection. My response was fairly similar to what I've already written, and then I spoke about nine-week assessments. At that interview, however, no one asked me how I would go about starting such a program in the school. Often, there's a real gap between having an idea and making it happen. For me, making an idea happen starts with good communication, and that's what I focused on once I became principal of Johnson Williams Middle School.

By mid-July of that first year, I had the opportunity to begin working on school improvement with an excellent team of department chairs. During meetings, we had open conversations about traditional exams, which had been given for a long time, and the frustrations teachers felt toward them, such as writing and grading them, losing valuable instructional time and moving on without analyzing what kinds of support students required. Hoping to stimulate conversation, I explained the nine-week diagnostic assessment model.

Fortunately, several of my department chairs were members of the committee that interviewed me, and they were already enthusiastic.

The key point I wanted to make to the department chairs was that this program was diagnostic. It was a way for teachers to increase conversations, improve student learning, and at the same time, improve student performance on state tests. I also pointed out that the program depended on an aligned curriculum, which would take time to develop. I tempered their enthusiasm with the fact that the model in place at my old school, Warren County Junior High School, had taken four years to perfect. It would take time for Johnson Williams Middle School to reach that point. The key thing was to start such a program.

ASSESSING YOUR SCHOOL'S JOURNEY TO NINE-WEEK ASSESSMENTS

Whether you're a new principal or a veteran in your school, it's helpful to investigate nine-week assessments by creating a list of strengths and weaknesses and then from these cull a list of areas to work on that are related to implementing nine-week assessments. Here's what I learned about the strengths and weaknesses of the faculty at Johnson Williams Middle School.

This information was for my assistants and me; I didn't share it with teachers, as I wanted to build their enthusiasm and not dampen it. I also wanted teachers and department chairs to see the challenges on their own. I've found that trying to circumvent problems by explaining potential issues up front is not that effective. If you have the luxury of time, let staff find the problems on their own and work to take ownership of the solutions. However, being aware of potential pitfalls is helpful to a principal when staff raises questions. I never take the route of *I told you so* or *If you had listened to me, this wouldn't have happened.* My role as principal is to guide the process and help everyone see the issues. This takes more time, but I believe it can build a stronger commitment to and understanding of the initiative.

By the end of our summer school improvement meetings, departments had adopted nine-week assessments. We had agreed on creating and administering the assessments, working out the kinks, and making adjustments. This is an excellent example of how continuous improvement can result when teachers and administrators work as a team on a school-wide initiative. Teamwork is a powerful force because it fosters the gathering, understanding, and sharing of information among the entire school community. I again cautioned faculty that it would take three to four years for the initiative to reach full effectiveness and for everyone to feel confident in their ability to create and analyze the assessments.

As teachers gradually transform exams into nine-week assessments, they need to continue assessing and evaluating students on a weekly basis so they can respond to their students' needs.

5: Ongoing Weekly Performance-Based Assessments Inform Instruction

Research shows that when teachers use performance-based or formative assessments to plan instruction, they can meet the needs of all learners immediately (Allington, 2006; Leahy, Lyon, Thompson, William, 2005; McTighe & O'Conner, 2005; Robb, 2006; Shepard, 2005). Frequent assessments can support teachers' decisions about what to reteach and cumulatively review as well as help them plan timely interventions and scaffolds that support students' learning (Black & Wiliam, 1998; Boston, 2002; Fuchs, Fuchs, Hamlett, Phillips, & Bentz, 1992). So you can see that frequent formative assessments can improve students' understanding and achievement because they receive help quickly. If schools are to reach their diverse populations, they can't afford to wait for the results of standardized, mandated tests. By the time those test results come in, the school year is over, and it's too late to help students effectively.

At my school, grade-level teams discuss their observations of students in diverse learning situations. These teachers understand that observing students' behavior and reactions to learning can tell them a great deal about students' feelings and levels of understanding. For example, a sixth grader tried to chat with a neighbor or asked to be excused whenever the teacher presented a new math concept. The team discovered that this student's behavior pattern also surfaced during mini-lessons in all subjects. The team developed several possible interventions:

- Asking the student why he avoided listening to teacher demonstrations.
- Keeping the student close to the front of the room.
- Working side by side with the student to make sure he understood the lesson.
- Pairing the student with a supportive peer during class practice.
- Offering extra help before or after school.

The team decided that if none of these interventions created progress, then the teachers would invite the student's parents to confer with them and discuss the option of additional educational testing.

In addition to careful, objective observations, ongoing assessments include evaluating journal work, writing, quizzes, tests, partner and small-group discussions, and conferring with students. You can show how important formative assessments are to you and your assistants by sitting in on team meetings and encouraging teachers to bring samples of students' work. Studying written work can provide insights into students' thinking processes, comprehension, and writing skill. By continually studying assessments, teachers generate topics for mini-lessons and, most importantly, discover which students can go on and which require reteaching and support.

Once teachers and department chairs were on board and working on developing nine-week assessments and using frequent formative assessments to plan instruction, it was time to make sure that all faculty members were keeping abreast of best-practice strategies so they would have the tools to plan instruction and interventions.

6: Best-Practice Strategies Improve Instruction and Learning

Even if a teacher studies research-tested reading and writing strategies in groups at school, learns about them at conferences, or observes other teachers using them with students, there is no guarantee that she will embrace these strategies and bring them to her students. What I have found effective with teachers who are committed to trying a strategy is a combination of reading and discussion. They share what they've done with colleagues during a team or department meeting or a full faculty meeting. Doing so provides teachers with feedback and support for questions they might have, and it's a way to move them beyond the study phase to doing it.

Here's how department chairs or team leaders, and the principal and his assistants, can deepen teachers' knowledge and use of best-practice strategies (Beck & McKeown, 2006; Harvey & Goudvis, 2000; Keene & Zimmermann, 1997; Robb, 2000, 2006; Tierney & Readence, 2000).

Develop a common language for these strategies: To avoid confusing students, it's important to develop a common language that could eventually be part of building-wide consistencies. Whether in history, science, math, or language arts, teachers should use the three-part learning framework: before learning, during learning, and after learning. Using common names for these strategies supports students' absorption of them. This can be completed during August work week before school opens, or you can organize a summer committee to develop a list that faculty will review and revise. (Summer committees need to be paid for their time so your decision will depend on available funds.)

Choose books to study and organize groups: Invite your librarian and teachers from all subjects to submit titles of books to study. It's important for content teachers to read books within their subjects as well as books on discipline and motivation that apply to all subjects. In Appendix N, on page 187, I've included a list of books and articles you and your teachers can investigate.

Each year, you'll want to review the latest Scholastic Professional Books catalog and catalogs from Heinemann, Stenhouse, ASCD, and Christopher-Gordon with your teachers. Reading about and using new strategies with students encourages teachers to adjust their toolbox of skills and their theory of learning.

Continue to revisit and study: Give your teachers and yourself the gift of time and know that studying, sharing, and revisiting strategies is an ongoing process. It's important to note that the teachers' learning journey is continual when professional study becomes a part of your school's culture. Without ongoing study, mutual support among faculty, and regular invitations to experts to come to your school to conduct workshops, any initiative falters and eventually fades away.

Part of the challenge of any principal's job is getting the most impact building wide with an initiative. Yes, I could have opted to send out a memo with a list of strategies that teachers had to use. Such a decision would have doomed the initiative to failure. Investing time up front, having a vision and carving out the time for teachers to have ongoing conversations surrounding that vision so they know they are part of the process can and will lead to success.

Continue to Think About . . .

Effective leadership includes helping your faculty take ownership of a program. The effective principal accepts the challenge of building commitment for new initiatives rather than resorting to the quick fix of a mandate. Developing a commitment and inspiring your faculty to care takes time. However, it's time well spent because including teachers in planning programs increases their desire to implement and evaluate them. Now, before moving to the next chapter, take a moment to evaluate your leadership style and how it impacts others by reflecting on the following questions:

- How could I have improved a recent initiative that I worked on?
- Am I comfortable with divergent opinions? How do I demonstrate that I am?
- How am I actively championing new initiatives?
- What am I doing to foster positive relationships and trust?
- What am I doing to improve instruction and students' achievement?

Chapter 6

Getting the Word Out:

Communication, the Principal's Beacon

● ● ●

*On the wall of my room when I was in rehab was a picture
of the space shuttle blasting off, autographed by every
astronaut now at NASA. On the top of the picture it says,
"We found nothing is impossible."
That should be our motto.*

- Christopher Reeve

T he science teacher, a member of the seventh-grade team that I was part of, poked his head in my room and asked, "Did you hear about the meeting this afternoon at three thirty? It should only last twenty to thirty minutes."

"No," I replied. I chuckled as I straightened up the piles of students' papers on my teacher's desk, thinking he was teasing.

"I'm serious," he said as he walked up to my desk. "Didn't you check your e-mail during lunch? We have to meet with parents who disagree with their daughter being placed in your extra-support literacy class."

"No," I answered. "I had cafeteria duty, and I taught back-to-back language arts classes all afternoon. I was just about to check it." I could feel irritation and frustration building in me. I had a dentist's appointment at four. I'd have to cancel, and it would be several weeks until I could get a new appointment. "I'll be down in a few minutes," I told the science teacher. Then I muttered to myself, "Everything around this place is done at the last minute. Why can't our principal be better organized?"

Similar situations occur in all schools. As a seventh-grade teacher, I did not fully understand the pressure parents could put on a principal. Today, after years of being a principal, I understand that there are times when calling a last-minute meeting cannot be avoided. However, a better way to inform teachers is for the principal or his assistants to speak personally to each teacher involved in the meeting to make sure that no one needs to be excused due to a pressing commitment. Moreover, when communication is working in a school, one or two last-minute meetings won't vex teachers. Teachers, other school staff, and parents appreciate a consistent, high level of communication from the principal.

There are many communication options open to you, and in this final chapter, I'll address some that I believe can construct a positive and productive school culture in which all school staff and parents rally around school projects and initiatives. My preference is to be as communicative as possible, for it sends the message that I value everyone's time, personal lives, and out-of-school commitments as well as their input and feedback.

This final chapter explores four ways to bolster communication at your school. Informal meetings over lunch or before school starts are the ideal way to learn about parents' and teachers' needs and problems or to discuss parent issues with your assistants. You'll also explore the benefits of having a school newsletter and Web site as well as guidelines and tips for organizing both. I'll show you the importance of creating telephone-answering procedures with your secretaries and all staff. And finally, we'll look at reviewing your school safety plan.

1. Communicating Through Informal Meetings

When you meet with school community members in informal settings, conversations are relaxed and personal, enabling you to discover important information that might never have emerged in more structured situations.

I frequently sit with small groups of teachers during lunch, eat with them, and listen carefully. I always let them set the chat agenda. Discussions might range from a great movie, book, or restaurant to a specific school situation.

During one such lunch gathering, I listened to teachers talk about a language arts teacher whose child had recently been diagnosed with a chronic illness. The teacher wanted to take the child to a larger medical institution for a second opinion, but since this was her first year, she did not want to ask for special privileges. I tucked this information inside my memory and then met with both my assistants to explore ways of supporting her. From the lunch conversation, it seemed that this language arts teacher needed to be absent for more than a week. We agreed that using all her sick days was not an option, because she might need them to care for her child. My two assistants and I decided that we each would give three of our sick days to the teacher. Next, I called the teacher in for a conference, explained the reason for the meeting, and told her she had nine days with pay to get expert help for her daughter. Because of that informal lunch meeting, I discovered information that the teacher might never have shared with me. Not only did the teacher receive a paid leave, but my assistants and I, as well as volunteers from the English department, covered her language arts classes for six school days.

It's important for school administrators to be sensitive to the needs of teachers with children, especially young children. When a child is ill and running a fever, I know that a parent wants to be with his or her child. You can make that happen by telling department chairs to see you when such a need arises. Either you or one of your assistants can cover a teacher's classes for part of the day. Supporting your teachers and staff by recognizing that they have vital needs outside of their job reduces their anxiety and tension and creates a positive workplace environment.

For me, part of the principal's job is to support every member of the school community, to show empathy and compassion, and to give back to teachers in need by inviting everyone to participate. That's why I also meet with my custodial and secretarial staff over a cup of coffee either before school starts or it ends. The message that I hope I'm sending is that I value their contributions, and I respect them personally. Again, I often discover information I might never know if I confined my interactions to formal, calendar meetings.

Helping and supporting families whose children attend your school tells them that you care about all your students and their families. From one of my secretaries, I discovered that the father of one of our students had lost his job. Struggling to make ends meet, this family couldn't pay their rent until he obtained another job. I sent a letter to staff asking anyone who could do so to help by contributing one to five dollars to help this family. Then I contacted their landlord and was able to anonymously pay part of the rent for three months. By then, the dad's new job had started.

Remember, you work with teachers who have needs beyond their roles at school and with families whose problems can affect their children's performance at school; by attending to these needs as much as you can, you model a way of treating people that can benefit any member of the community in need—even yourself.

I also urge you to reserve time to meet with small groups of students. This can include student leaders, class officers, and if your school is small enough, all students. Attend student government meetings, invite groups into your office two to three times a month during lunch, be visible in the halls, and talk to students throughout the day. Seeing the school through your students' eyes can enable you to lead more effectively because students often have knowledge of one another's problems and of dangers that teachers and staff haven't observed. From students, I've learned about knives in students' lockers, students who needed counseling—potential problems that I headed off through meetings with the students and their families and referrals to guidance.

One or two mornings a month, I hold breakfast gathering for parents before school starts. I invite parents to have bagels and coffee with me and my assistants from 7:15 a.m. to 8:00 a.m. Some gatherings feature a department or a team or the custodial or secretarial staff; I include everyone to show that I value the contribution of all school community members. In a relaxed and informal setting, parents can chat candidly and raise questions about issues such as the curriculum, exams, assessments, and tutoring. It's a great way to understand the pulse of your parent body as well as to give them an opportunity to get to know the people who interact with their children each day.

2. Communicating Through a Newsletter and Web Site

I find that communicating with the members of my school community through a newsletter and a school Web site is also effective. Above all, keep in mind that newsletters and Web sites are reflections of your school so they need to be the best you can make them.

Before you organize a newsletter, ask yourself the following questions to help you plan more effectively and efficiently:

- Does the school already have a newsletter program in place? If so, have you looked over previous newsletters? Do you know how frequently parents received a copy?

- Who is responsible for putting the newsletter together? What was the previous principal's role?

- Who folds the newsletters and mails them out? Is there enough money in your budget to cover mass mailings?

Of course, if the school is new, the opportunity exists for you to start a newsletter as a new initiative. Even though I have been a principal for several years, I still review and reflect on these questions. Doing so enables me to continually evaluate and update procedures that are in place.

The Ins and Outs of Creating a Newsletter

An effective newsletter is visually clear and not too long, avoids excessive use of clip art, and contains important information for parents. The following guidelines will help you create a school newsletter that parents will look forward to receiving and reading:

Basic components: Standardize several sections of your newsletter. This creates consistency and makes it easy for readers to find information. I've found that parents appreciate a consistent format so they don't have to search for pertinent information. As the year progresses, you can add new sections. Below is a list of headings that will work for most schools.

- A Word From the Principal
- Dates to Remember
- Parent Advisory Corner
- Review of Parent Morning Meetings
- Athletic Report
- Guidance Corner
- Tips for Your Child's Success at School

You can add a section that spotlights one or more teachers. This works well if there are many new staff members, or you can put a team or department on center stage. Start small, and gradually add sections based on feedback you collect from teachers, from parents during breakfast gatherings, and from surveys and telephone calls. (See Appendix O, pp. 188–189, for a sample newsletter.)

Parents want to be informed about school issues and made aware of key dates, and a newsletter is an effective way to accomplish this. Given the choice, I always overcommunicate rather than undercommunicate—and remember that it takes time to find the balance between communicating too much and too little. Moreover, the balance point differs from school to school because it depends upon the specific needs of your parents and community. My key piece of advice is to keep in the forefront of your mind that your newsletter represents your school, as does your Web site.

Leadership Tip:
To Publish or Not to Publish a Newsletter Quickly

In the past, I've felt pressure to have a newsletter out quickly after the year starts. If you have an experienced staff to do this, then proceed. In my most recent position, I discovered that the head secretary had been doing the newsletters for years. She, along with the previous principal, had developed a format and a schedule for mailing them out. All that I needed to do in August of my first year was to produce the message from the principal. Also, I had access to newsletters from previous years so I was able to read the August messages from the last principal. However, if your school has never published a newsletter, the school's newsletter is poor, or you lack the support staff to publish one, then I advise you to avoid plunging in at the start of the year. Sending out a letter in August from you to the parents is enough. That will buy you the time you need to develop a newsletter schedule and gather support among staff.

A School Web Site: An Opportunity to Extend Communication

An exciting way to reach out to your parents and community is through a school Web site. More and more families have computer access, and a strong Web presence is a good way to represent your school and provide pertinent information. Your school is likely to fall into one of these three categories: it has no Web site; it has a reasonably good Web site that needs improvement; it has an excellent Web site. To rate your Web site, please review the following statements. The more you answer yes, the better your site.

- I have adequate technology support to run the school Web site.
- Our Web site is visually pleasing and contains photos of the school and staff.
- The language on our Web site is easy to read.
- Our Web site is easy to navigate.

- Parents can access daily announcements and other up-to-date information from our site.
- Parents and students can access homework assignments on our site.
- Pertinent information on all aspects of our school is easily available through the Web site.

If you answered no to most of the questions, then consider constructing a new Web site. Building a top-notch Web site requires planning, vision, and time. If you start in September, it will take at least six months to complete. A district-wide effort is the ideal way to go. It ensures consistency among school Web sites, so one school doesn't outshine another. If that kind of effort is not likely to be supported, then you may need to go it alone. (Hopefully, the central office will see the benefits of your Web site and require sites in all schools!)

The key to building a useful Web site is having a technology department that can provide technical assistance or a staff member with strong technology skills. If you don't have the technology support, you may need to hire an outside source. If your budget is tight, seek out a new company and negotiate a package you can afford. A state-of-the-art school Web site can be good publicity for a new tech company, especially if you commit to advertising their work to other school districts. With support staff in place, developing the Web site is your next step.

SUGGESTIONS FOR SETTING WEB SITE CONSTRUCTION IN MOTION

This section will assist you with organizing the effort to conceptualize or design your site and with creating its content. To initiate the process, announce through e-mail or at a faculty meeting that you're forming a Web site committee. Often, teachers feel they need technical skills to participate, but that's not the case. Let faculty know that your technology experts will design and launch the site but that you need your teachers to conceptualize it and create its content. Convey the skills that committee members will need to set the project in motion: They should be able to meet deadlines, write effectively, and be creative and artistic. In addition, teachers serving on this committee should have a strong belief that a Web site effort is a valuable project.

Organize the Effort Into Four Stages

By investing time in the planning stage to build consensus among faculty for the site's design and content and by moving forward slowly, you'll accomplish your goals of creating a site that informs all members of your school community. Whether people use the site frequently depends on its quality, links, and the continuous updating of information. The model I've proposed below is inclusive and takes time. The result, however, will be a site that strongly represents a school's values, goals, and mission. You can explore the Web site for my school, Johnson-Williams Middle School, at http://jwms.clarke.k12.va.us/.

Stage 1: Research successful Web sites. Be sure to set aside enough time to review other successful sites. As committee members review these sites, ask them to jot down what they liked, such as the links to departments or daily homework assignments, as well as what they didn't like, such as links that are tough to access. The review should include education, community, corporate, and nonprofit Web sites. I've found that some of the best Web sites are outside of the education field. Committee members should report on the excellent features they discovered when reviewing other Web sites. Each person should share his or her review of what made the Web site outstanding.

Create timelines for gathering the information, but make sure you give teachers enough time to complete this stage. Then schedule several follow-up meetings so committee members can share their observations and work toward framing what the main page of your school's Web site will look like. I suggest you meet in the computer lab so teachers can show one another the sites they rated as excellent.

Stage 2: Schematics make the layout and design of your site inviting. The look of your Web site can be inviting or send the message that the school staff didn't put much effort into creating it. Committee members should determine the kinds of headings and drop-downs and visuals they want and where these will be placed. Drop-downs are vertical lists that appear when the cursor clicks on or moves over a header. For example, under the header "Physical Education" there might be a list of all the sports your school offers or the sports offered by season.

Next, the committee works as a group to recommend Web site components to integrate into the school's layout. Before reporting back to staff, committee members should generate a list of headings, information contained under each heading, and all the links they want the site to have. This stage can take as long as three to four weeks to complete, depending on the number of headings and links.

Stage 3: Meet the challenges of writing the Web site's content. Once you've planned the site, the next challenge is to gather information for the content and write it. The committee meets and divides writing the content among its members. Creating good content as a group can be tricky because everyone has a different voice and writing style. I suggest that two committee members who are strong writers edit the content for consistency. Listed below are some guidelines for creating the site's content.

- Set a specific date for content to be turned in to you or to the administrator in charge.
- Place content in Word format.
- Check content for grammar, syntax errors, and consistency.
- Pass all content to the two designated members in charge of editing for consistency of style and voice.

Stage 4: Review and revise the content. The two designated members should read the content to make sure it meets the established criteria. At this stage, the page should be conceptualized with schematics in place and content completed. Now your technology department or an outside source can create the site. When the Web site is completed, set aside about three weeks for committee members and faculty to review the site's home page, navigate through the various pages and links, and provide written feedback. Next, at a faculty meeting, discuss any suggestions and work with your tech staff to incorporate them into the site. Finally, invite student leaders to review the site and offer suggestions from their perspective. Run these by teachers and ask your tech staff to add teacher-approved student suggestions to the site and officially launch it.

CLOSING THOUGHTS ON WEB SITE CONSTRUCTION

Once the Web site has been launched, invite staff to brainstorm creative ways to market it and increase usage. Some ideas that have worked in my school are putting the Web site address on report cards and school letterhead and posting it in all classrooms. If you have the capability to post daily announcements to be posted or scroll updated information on the site, a staff member will need to be trained to do so. This may warrant additional salary, but it's well worth it, for the school's ability to communicate with the community will increase dramatically.

The beauty of Web sites is that information is available from any location with Internet access. I had a parent who frequently traveled. He called me one day to say how happy he was that he could check his son's homework and read our daily announcements from California.

Calls like that make the effort worthwhile. However, calls come into a school all day long—and not all of them are as pleasant. Phone contact or a short discussion with a secretary in the front office is frequently the first communication parents have with your school. Your job is to ensure that these exchanges, whether on the phone or in person, are positive and affirming for parents and staff.

3. Evaluating Your School's Telephone Responses and Front Office Communication

I've called colleague's schools and been greeted with a gruff hello or a well thought-out response such as, "Smithson School. Good morning, how can I help you?" The first response made me want to hang up; the second set an upbeat and positive tone. Your front office staff members are the ones who set this tone so pay attention to how they answer the telephone and greet parents and students who visit the office. Poor telephone etiquette can mean losing a parent's support or prompting a parent to complain about the front office staff to his friends. Discussing telephone communication and face-to-face communication is easier if you're a new principal than if you've been in a school for a few years and are trying to effect change. Your secretaries may feel their communication skills were good enough before and wonder why they have to change them now.

Few school divisions require job training for new office staff or refresher training for established staff, so communicating thoughts about answering the telephone and speaking to parents, visitors, and students in the front office will be your responsibility. Whether you're a new or a veteran principal, it's important for you to be sensitive to the feelings of your office staff when instituting changes. The desire to change should come from several discussions over coffee and lunch. Avoid directives; work to build consensus through conversations. It's equally important for you and your administrative team to model the kind of responses you hope staff will adopt. In other words, lead by example. Use what you do as a springboard for discussions, and use their personal experiences as well.

To initiate a discussion of phone etiquette, I ask staff to reflect on phone contacts they've had with hotels, businesses, or restaurants. How were they treated? If the contact was pleasant and positive, how did it make them feel? If the person was rude and abrupt, what impression did that give? In this initial meeting, I also share my own experiences.

Suggestions for Improving Telephone and Front Office Communication

Review the following guidelines for involving secretaries in the change process and adjust them to meet your school's needs:

- Provide time for secretaries to meet without you so they can converse freely in order to agree upon and establish some uniform expectations for phone usage.
- Set a tight timeline of two to four meetings within a one- to two-week period with your secretaries. (Include the dates and time of each meeting in the timeline. As a first-time principal, I made the mistake of not establishing timelines and the meetings never occurred.)
- Offer the following discussion items for staff to focus on during the first meeting:
  1. Discuss their areas of strength and the areas that they feel need improvement.
  2. Consider setting some customer-service standards for the office, especially telephone etiquette.

I let my secretaries know that I, too, will work on suggestions for answering the telephone and bring examples of how other schools respond to callers to our next meeting. The goal at the next meeting will be for all of us to look at the information we've gathered and formulate standards. Again, your success with changing or fine-tuning telephone and front office communication will be greater if you involve your staff in developing the changes and new standards.

Guidelines for School Telephone Etiquette and Face-to-Face Communication

The office staff in my previous school created these 13 guidelines, laminated them, and posted them by every office phone. They are simple, create consistency, and provide the positive focus you want.

1. Attempt to answer the phone promptly—within three rings.
2. Be alert: A cheerful, wide-awake greeting sets an upbeat tone.
3. Be expressive: Speak at a moderate rate and volume; vary the tone of your voice.
4. Keep your language simple.
5. Show that you are genuinely interested in the other person's needs.
6. Be polite; this builds confidence in our school.
7. Always ask permission to place a person on hold.
8. Check in frequently if there's a caller waiting on the line. Thank the caller for waiting.
9. Always be discreet. Never say the principal is on a coffee break or hasn't come in yet.
10. Keep a writing utensil and paper by the phone or the office counter to take messages.
11. Thank the person for their call or for coming into the school and checking with the office.
12. When ending a call, let the caller hang up first.
13. Avoid letting a visitor, parent, or student wait too long in the office. Communicate as quickly as possible or explain that you will be with him or her in a few minutes.

Rather than giving this list to your staff, start the process of having them develop their own list. Suggest that they call other schools to gather information on telephone etiquette. Make sure you also budget time for them to converse and share their experiences and to collaborate to improve their telephone communication systems.

It's also imperative for you to develop and plan procedures for visitors that will keep students and staff safe. In today's climate, it's essential that you and your entire staff continually review and revise safety procedures and communicate with one another on these issues. When children, teachers, and other staff arrive at your school, they should feel safe so they can do their jobs well.

4. Safety and Your School

A safe school must be an administrative and staff priority. If you're a new principal, speak with other principals in your district to ensure that you're doing the required drills. Also, if you have any safety questions, make sure you ask a colleague to find out possible answers. Being proactive will make things easier in the long run. With safety issues, continual communication among all staff, students, and parents and constant vigilance should be one of your highest priorities.

What can you do as principal to assure a safe school environment? New principals must understand the procedures for their school's safety system; veterans should know the safety system and set goals to improve it yearly. Another part of school safety is knowing where students are at all times, which can be a challenge in large schools. If students can easily report late to classes or take bathroom breaks, you can be giving them the opportunity to cause trouble that will affect them and others.

The questions and responses that follow summarize the discussions I've had on the subject of safety with other principals. Review them, and reflect on your own situation. How would you respond to each question?

How accessible is your school during the day? Are numerous doors open for people to enter the school?
Our school has only one door open during the school day. This is a door located at the front entrance of the school. We have a sign posted asking all visitors to please report to the main office. The main office is immediately visible on the right as you enter the school.

Is there a surveillance system to monitor access areas?

We have a surveillance system in the school. I have our school resource officer monitor the cameras. If there are any suspicious occurrences, she reports them directly to me, noting the location and time.

Are administrators and teachers highly visible in the halls in the morning, at dismissal, and when classes change?

In the past this was an issue. Teachers weren't in the hall during class changes. Now they stand at their doors to assist with monitoring the hall and to greet students as they enter their classrooms. This has assisted with tardies. Also, each administrator has a designated area to monitor in the morning, at dismissal, and during class changes.

Are duty stations effective and consistently covered? Are expectations written out so staff understands each duty?

At the end of each year, we have an administrative discussion about our duty areas. We discuss what went well and what can be adjusted for the next year. Our goal is to cover areas of the school that need a high level of supervision. For example, we have had an increase in the number of students who are picked up by their parents. As a result, we had to add an additional teacher to supervise our car rider area. We have written expectations for all duties along with a question-and-answer section that covers the typical issues that arise. Finally, we overlap our duties by one day. This allows the current duty teacher to work with the new teacher for a day to clear up any questions.

Have procedures been created for fire drills, high-wind drills, and lockdowns?

We have procedures for all these drills. We have one fire drill per month, and we record the amount of time it takes to clear and secure the school. Also, we do two high-wind drills and three lockdown drills each year. We have written procedures for each of these drills, and we communicate them to teachers through e-mails and by placing hard copies in their mailboxes. We require teachers to post these procedures on a bulletin board in their classrooms.

Does the school have clear procedures for students being in the hall during class, including consistent student bathroom procedures?

We communicate to students our expectations that they should be in class on time. We do this in several ways: At the start of the year, my assistants meet with each grade level to review the student handbook, and teachers follow up with class reviews. We have several expectations for bathroom breaks. First, we don't allow breaks during the first four minutes or the last four minutes of class. If a student is ill and needs immediate attention, the teacher can call the nurse and me or one of my assistants if I'm unavailable. Students who go on a bathroom break must have a signed break notebook with them while they're in the hall. This serves as a log for teachers to see if the student is taking far too many breaks or is on break when she should be in class. Finally, we communicate to staff that only one student at a time should leave the room. Exceptions do arise, but they are unusual.

Has data been kept on student tardies to class? How can this be improved?

In the past, we would have teachers record the number of tardies and report the data to the administration. This was the reason we asked staff to stand by their doorways at change time. Their presence reduced tardies. Teachers do still record tardies. Now, though, if a student accumulates four tardies in nine weeks, he is referred to the assistant principal for discussions to discover the reasons for these tardies and to figure out ways to prevent them.

Establish Clear Visitor Procedures

● ● ●

No one wants to send the message that his or her school is not a welcoming place, but to assure everyone's safety, you'll need to find a balance. Some schools have checkpoints for visitors/parents to show identification upon entry. That requires a staff member to be at a set post, which is often not practical.

I recommend that you lock all doors except the door that leads to the front office. Then you can have signs posted at locked entrance areas that read, "Visitors, please report to the office." (Notice the word please. Many schools use the word *must* instead of *please*. Word choice can send a friendly welcoming message or a restrictive one.) Upon entry to the

Leadership Tip:
Raise Staff's Awareness of Strangers

Communicate to all staff members that if they see an unfamiliar person in the building without a visitor sticker they should politely ask the person if they can assist him. Sometimes, people can bypass the office, especially if things are busy. A staff member should ask the person to go to the office immediately and then call the office to apprise you or your secretary of the situation. Don't argue with someone who doesn't want to cooperate. Immediately call the office for help.

front office, the visitor is asked by the secretary for identification and the purpose of the visit. Most of the time, a visit has been prearranged.

Unexpected visits to staff by parents are inappropriate; parents should never interrupt a class. If a parent must see a teacher, she should leave a message for the teacher to call. Most often this can be done through the secretary. There will be times when an angry parent demands to see a teacher immediately, and you may need to defuse the situation by attempting to calm the parent. I've found that if I assure the parent that I will personally ask the teacher to contact her, he calms down. There will be times, however, when you'll need to drop what you're doing and spend additional time with a disgruntled parent.

When visiting is appropriate, the parent should sign in and be issued a visitor badge or sticker.

Finally, safety can be an excellent topic for a committee to study. It can evaluate the school, survey staff, or do a safety audit of the facility. The committee can provide recommendations to the administrative team. You need to continually examine and evaluate your systems in order to maintain the highest possible level of safety.

Continue to Think About ...

Being a principal who considers the needs of all school community members requires long hours of work, ongoing professional study on instruction and discipline, and honing your communication skills. You set your school's tone and culture and are responsible for every student and staff member.

Before closing this book, reflect on the questions that follow. They can heighten the communication between you and your staff; keep you focused on creating an environment that fosters learning, thinking, and problem solving for teachers and students; and help you make parents an integral part of your community.

- Am I exploring how others perceive me as a communicator? Can I accept and act on a need to change?
- Do I delegate responsibilities among my assistants and teachers and follow up to make sure deadlines have been met?
- Do I respect the fact that students are at different learning levels and support teachers as they try to meet students' needs?
- Is safety a priority at my school? How am I helping everyone take responsibility for one another's safety?
- Do I listen carefully to all members of the school community and welcome diverse ideas and opinions?
- Do parents participate in our school?
- Do I meet often and informally with parents, teachers, and students so we can get to know one another on a personal level?
- Am I considering everyone's needs and finding ways to help parents, teachers, and students who have problems that the school can help solve?

Bibliography of Professional Books and Articles

Allington, R. L. (2006). Fluency: Still waiting after all these years. In S. J. Samuels and A. E. Farstrup (Eds.), *What research has to say about fluency instruction*. Newark, DE: International Reading Association.

Beck, I. L. & McKeown, M. G. (2006). *Improving comprehension with questioning the author*. New York: Scholastic.

Black, P., & Wiliam, D. (1998a). Assessment and classroom learning. *Assessment in Education*, 5(1), 7–74.

Black, P., & Wiliam, D. (1998b). Inside the black box: Raising standards through classroom achievement. *Phi Delta Kappan, 80*(2), 139–148.

Bonstingl, J. J. (2001). *Schools of quality*. Thousand Oaks, CA: Corwin Press.

Boston, C. (2002). The concept of formative assessment. *Practical Assessment, Research and Evaluation, 8*(9). Retrieved July 13, 2006, from http://pareonline.net/getvn.asp?v=8&n=9

Covey, Stephen R. (1990). *The 7 habits of highly effective people*. New York: Free Press.

Fuchs, L. S., Fuchs, D., Hamlett, C. L., Phillips, N. B., & Bentz, J. (1994). Classwide curriculum-based measurement: Helping general educators meet the challenge of student diversity. *Exceptional Children, 60*, 518–537.

Harvey, S., & Goudvis, A. (2000). *Strategies that work: Teaching comprehension to enhance understanding*. York, ME: Stenhouse.

Herman, J. L. & Baker, E.L. (2006). Making benchmark testing work. *Educational Leadership, 63*(3), 48–55.

Keene, E. O., & Zimmermann, S. (1997). *Mosaic of thought*. Portsmouth, NH: Heinemann.

Leahy, S., Lyon, C., Thompson, M., & William, D. (2006). Classroom assessment: Minute by minute, day by day. *Educational Leadership, 63*(3), 18–25.

Marshall, M. (2001). *Discipline without stress punishments or rewards*. Los Alamitos, CA: Piper Press.

Marzano, R. J. (2004). *Building background knowledge for academic achievement: Research on what works in school*. Alexandria, VA: Association for Supervision and Curriculum Development.

McTighe, J., & O'Conner, K. (2006). Seven practices for effective learning. *Educational Leadership*, 63(3), 10–17.

Robb, L. (2000a). *Redefining staff development: A collaborative model for teachers and administrators*. Portsmouth, NH: Heinemann.

Robb, L. (2000b). *Teaching reading in middle school: A strategic approach to teaching reading that improves comprehension and thinking*. New York: Scholastic.

Robb, L. (2006c). *Teaching reading: A complete guide for grades 4 and up*. New York: Scholastic.

Shepard, L. A. (2005). Linking formative assessment to scaffolding. *Educational Leadership, 63*(3): 66–71.

Sheppard, B. (1996). *Exploring the transformational nature of instructional leadership*. The Alberta Journal of Educational Research, 42(4), 32–34.

Tierney, R. J., & Readence, J. E. (2000). *Reading strategies and practices: A compendium*. Boston: Allyn and Bacon.

A. Parent Volunteer Sign-Up Form

Use this form at your first Meet the Principal gathering. You can also adapt it for use throughout the year.

DEAR PARENTS: We need your assistance in our school. We encourage you to volunteer!

FUND-RAISING COMMITTEE

Name   Phone number   E-mail address

_____

_____

ACADEMIC COMMITTEE

Name   Phone number   E-mail address

_____

_____

HOSPITALITY COMMITTEE

Name   Phone number   E-mail address

_____

_____

LIBRARY VOLUNTEERS

Name   Phone number   E-mail address

_____

_____

B. Procedures for Purchasing and Ordering Supplies

I communicate procedures for reimbursement and placing purchase orders with this memo. Each staff member receives a copy, and I follow up with team leaders and department chairs to explain the procedures and the rationale behind each one. Notice that I am the person who approves purchasing. If I allowed my assistants to approve purchases also, I would be creating two huge problems for myself:

● It takes time to find out what purchases other administrators have approved.

● Sharing purchasing approval may make is possible for some staff members to take advantage of an administrator, especially one who says yes too often.

PROCEDURES FOR PURCHASING AND ORDERING SUPPLIES
GENERAL PURCHASING PROCEDURES

● *All* purchases should be preapproved by Mr. Robb. Please understand that we will not reimburse you for purchases made without prior approval.

● Get a *purchase order form* from the bookkeeper and fill it out completely.

● Turn in completed purchase order to bookkeeper. She will give it to Mr. Robb to sign.

● Once it is approved, the purchase order will be copied and faxed to the vendor.

● When your order arrives, please check it immediately to see if you have received everything. Also, return all packing slips to the bookkeeper immediately. Indicate if your order is complete or incomplete, and sign and date the packing slips. Payment cannot be made without the proof of the packing slip.

REQUEST FOR REIMBURSEMENT

● Get written approval from Mr. Robb, and then purchase only the items approved.

● Bring the receipts to the bookkeeper for reimbursement. Again, only the items approved by Mr. Robb in advance will be paid.

You will be reimbursed by check on the 1st or the 15th of that month.

C. Letter to Team Leader or Department Chair for Allocation of Money

School budgets often contain a significant amount of money for instructional supplies. Sending letters that tell departments how much money they've been allocated and how much time they have to spend it gives you control over the process. If this is not done, requests will come in randomly, making it more difficult to track the speed and equity of spending. There is no way to completely control spending, as random expenses will occur. In a typical school year I allocate money in three cycles.

In the letter that follows, the amount allocated can vary. To achieve some consistency, I use a figure based on the amount of my budget and the members in a department: $200 per teacher. The dollar amount will vary depending on your school's budget.

Setting a deadline for turning in orders is very helpful. Setting a date gets things moving, and it also demonstrates that timelines need to be adhered to if the school is to function at a high level.

Dear_____,

I am allocating $1,000.00 for your department to spend on instructional supplies. Please meet with your department in order to assess the needs of members.

Have all your orders turned in to our bookkeeper by October 15. If your orders are not in by that date, the money will be allocated to a different department.

If I can be of any assistance, please let me know. I appreciate your efforts as department chair. Keep up the good work.

— E. Robb

D. Back to School Night

Suggestions and Guidelines for the Principal's Speech

The principal's speech on Back to School Night should be kept short. Parents come to walk the school and meet teachers, not to hear a lengthy speech.

If you are a new principal, begin by introducing yourself. Let parents and students know that you are excited about being principal and that you look forward to meeting them. Give an overview of the evening, including the end time.

If embellished, the seven points listed below can be turned into a five- to ten-minute speech. (They are adapted from *The 7 Habits of Highly Effective People* by Stephen Covey.) Each point can be expanded by relating a personal story. Close by thanking parents for their attendance. After my speech, I turn the assembly over to a designated staff member to continue the program.

Here is an example of an outline I've used for a Back to School Night speech.

TOPIC: Habits for School Success

1. **Be proactive:** Take responsibility for your schooling; do your best.
2. **Begin with the end in mind:** Set some goals for yourself: better grades, getting involved with a club or athletics.
3. **Put first things first:** Learn the benefits of prioritizing. For students, this speaks to the balance of doing your best in school along with having fun.
4. **Think win-win:** Never win at another's expense. Find ways that everyone can experience success.
5. **Seek first to understand, then to be understood:** Improve your listening skills. This will help you to better understand others and enhance your school experience.
6. **Be team focused:** This is not for athletes only. Teams can be classrooms, clubs, or even our school. Working together, everyone achieves more.
7. **Have fun:** School should be enjoyable. I encourage and challenge all students to become active members of this student body. I guarantee that it will increase your enjoyment of school.

Suggested Topics for a PowerPoint Presentation

These suggestions are most appropriate for a middle school, but you can adjust them for elementary or high school.

- **If your school is small, introduce grade-level teachers by making and showing a slide for each one.**
- **If your school is large, begin with a slide for each team. List the teachers on each team. Introduce only the team leader.**
- **Have slides for elective teachers.**
- **Daily schedule:** Create a slide describing the school schedule: when classes begin, lunch, dismissal, and so on. If your school has staggered dismissal, this is an appropriate time to explain that.
- **Lunchroom procedures:** On this slide, include the cost of breakfast and lunch and other necessary information, such as à la carte items, prepayment, and charges.
- **Helpful hints:** Present information about how the school communicates, such as homework hotlines, Web sites, the school newspaper, e-mails, the newsletter, and how students receive messages if parents call. Also include information about lockers. The list can go on and on, but keep it short and informative.
- **After-school activities:** Display information on clubs, after-school programs, and athletics.
- **Review of the first day of school:** This slide tells students where to report and how you're going to handle students who do not have a schedule.
- **If traffic flow is an issue, show a slide that explains how to enter the school to pick up a student.**
- **Student schedules:** Block schedules can be confusing since most are odd/even. Explain the schedule clearly on a slide. If you're having parents follow their child's block schedule, decide in advance if they will do an even day first and then an odd day, or go straight through.
- **School map:** The last slide can be a map of the school. Plan ahead and have these copied for parents to pick up as they begin their tour. Place the maps on a table or several tables if the school is large.

E. Presenting Your School's Annual Goals

During the month of August, I review conversations I've had with teachers, other principals, central office administrators, and additional building staff. These topics are always on top of my reflection list: professional study, a commitment to differentiating instruction, home-school relationships, ways to better support and honor faculty and staff, and exploring options for increasing after-school activities. Note that these goals all focus on the entire school and not one subject or grade. Moreover, if a school has not made AYP (Annual Yearly Progress) or has major deficiencies in standardized testing, then those should be included.

Next, I prioritize the list, narrowing it to four to five goals that I feel are reachable that year. Then, I communicate these to the central office, to our parent organization and advisory group, and of course, to faculty and staff.

A SUGGESTED LIST OF ANNUAL GOALS
Use these suggestions to formulate your own list.

- Increase professional development opportunities at school and opportunities for teachers to attend conferences.
- Continue studying differentiating instruction in all subject areas through professional development and book study.
- Invite teachers to plan one differentiated unit of study, then share their experiences with team and/or department members as well as the entire faculty.
- Survey students to discover their ideas for additional clubs and activities that could be offered after school. Find ways to support these extras with money and staff.
- Work with teachers on developing ideas for enlarging the home-school contact program.
- Work with the school leadership team, which may consist of administrative and grade-level teacher representation, to explore ways to celebrate successes in the entire school community.

F. Book Study Club

Guidelines for Book Studies

- Find a staff member to lead a book study. The principal should serve as a group member.
- Advertise the book study to get staff involved.
- Have an initial meeting to present an overview of the book and to "jigsaw" chapters.
- Explain expectations for presenting a chapter.
- Create a plan of implementation for new ideas.

Suggested Books

Allen, J. (2000). *Yellow brick road: Shared and guided paths to independent reading 4–12.* York, ME: Stenhouse.

Allington, R. (2001). *What really matters for struggling readers: Designing research-based programs.* New York: Longman.

Beck, I. L., & McKeown, M. G. (2006). *Improving comprehension with questioning the author.* New York: Scholastic.

Bonstingl, J. J. (2001). *Schools of quality.* Thousand Oaks, CA: Corwin Press.

Culham, R. (2003). *6 + 1 traits of writing: The complete guide, grades 3 and up.* New York: Scholastic.

Daniels, H. (2002). *Literature circles: Voice and choice in book clubs & reading groups.* York, ME: Stenhouse.

Marshall, M. (2001) *Discipline without stress punishments or rewards.* Los Alamitos, CA: Piper Press.

Robb, L. (2000). *Teaching reading in middle school.* New York: Scholastic.

Robb, L. (2003). *Teaching reading in social studies, science, and math.* New York: Scholastic.

Tomlinson, C. A. (1999). *The differentiated classroom: Responding to the needs of all learners.* Alexandria, VA: Association for Supervision and Curriculum Development.

Wilhelm, J. (2002). *Action strategies for deepening comprehension.* New York: Scholastic.

Wilhelm, J. (2005). *Reading is seeing.* New York: Scholastic.

Zarnowski, M. (2006). *Making sense of history: Using high-quality literature and hands-on experiences to build content knowledge.* New York: Scholastic.

Teacher-Led Book Study

Book studies are more effective when promoted by a teacher. Here's an example. Judy Martin e-mailed the following note to staff and also posted it in the teacher work room.

Teacher Facilitator: Judy Martin

You Can Improve Teacher-Student Relationships

Stop stressing when you discipline students. Internal motivation is a far more powerful and effective way to change behavior than punishments or rewards.

Discipline Without Stress, Punishments or Rewards by Marvin Marshall offers you a revolutionary way to reduce irresponsible behavior!

Read this book and you will learn how to

- improve teacher-student relationships;
- raise student responsibility; and
- promote learning.

Here's what nationally known educator Harry Wong says about Marshall's book:

"What should I do with this kid?" is the most common question I receive from readers of my book, and my in-service presentations.

I answer by saying that you do not do things to people. Rather, you need to teach people to do things for themselves. Classroom management teaches procedures for accomplishing this.

Choose either to jigsaw the book in one session or several sessions.

Discipline is a distinctly different subject. Discipline deals with how people behave, whereas procedures deal with how things are done.

Marvin Marshall has created a program that challenges many assumptions and practices used with today's young people. He clearly and concisely demonstrates how the external approaches of relying on rules, imposing consequences, rewarding students for appropriate behavior, and punishing students to make them obey are all counterproductive.

This landmark book is a must read whether you are a starting or experienced teacher. You will find each chapter full of insights and strategies that will improve your influence and effectiveness with others.

If you're interested, here's how to obtain a copy of this book:

Ten of Dr. Marshall's books have been purchased by the front office. Please e-mail me if you are interested in joining our book study. Mr. Robb assures me that professional development points can be earned from this activity. We all are formulating goals for this year. A book study on effective classroom management can be an excellent goal. Please e-mail me if you are interested in this venture. When names are in, we will have an initial meeting to discuss how we will proceed.

G. Types of School Goals

Administrative Goals: These are "macro" goals that focus all staff members in several key areas. They are to build common language, add structure, and form a bridge for all departments in the school.

Instructional Goals: Continue our school's focus on quarterly assessments and data desegregation with a heightened focus on using data to improve instruction and student learning. Our school will continue to focus on professional development to improve our use of instructional methods, differentiating of instruction, and writing across the curriculum.

SMART Goals: We as a school will focus on creating specific goals that use the SMART acronym: specific, measurable, attainable, realistic, and timely. Specific goals will be an expectation for all team and department plans. This year we will encourage staff to teach students how to create specific goals for their learning.

Goals That Serve Our Entire Community: As a staff, we recognize that we exist to serve students, parents, and the community at large. Each team will set specific goals for parent contact and communication. Also, each staff member will complete two home visits this year. Our front office staff will create a customer-service plan that includes phone etiquette, professional dress, and the completion of a newsletter every quarter. Additionally, we have set a goal to post daily announcements on our school Web site.

Data Goals: Establish data goals for organizational effectiveness and develop a system to manage the data. This focus on data will allow our school to look at key performance indicators and set goals for improvement. A data team will be established to create a list of key school indicators, and timelines will be established for collecting and reporting data.

If you are asked to present your goals to a larger group, the above format can be used to create an overhead that you can use as a springboard for speaking. It also makes an excellent handout for listeners to use as you present.

H. Welcome-Back Letters

Summer Letter to School Department Chair or Instructional Team Leader

Dear_____,

    I hope your summer is going well. I am delighted that we have completed a successful year, and I am sure the upcoming year will be the same. I realize that you are ready to review and update your improvement plan. To assist and guide your efforts, please review the guidelines given below.

    When you format goals, please construct them in SMART goal format. The attached sheet outlines the structure.

    During our work week, we will meet to review test data. We will be working on packets that have the following:

- State testing scores and grading correlation by department: Several times last year we discussed that a C in a course should result in a pass on the state test. This may be an area to set a goal.
- Trend data on failures for the year: Data has been compiled to show trends over the last three years. Reductions in failures may be an area to set a goal.
- Item analysis per question: This data will allow you to see whole areas of group weakness, which may result in setting a curriculum alignment goal.
- AYP data: This data has been broken down into subgroups and their percentage of passing. Targeting these students with student improvement plans may be an area for a new goal.

    The supplied data will allow you to build additional specific goals. During the first part of the work week, we will set a date for when your final draft is due to me. Together, we'll review your goals. Then the plan will go to your department for adjustments that will lead to group consensus.

    Finally, I am looking forward to the opportunities for improvement that are ahead of us. You provided superb leadership for your department last year. I have great confidence that this will continue throughout the current year.

Sincerely,

Evan Robb

Principal, J.W.M.S.

Work Week Announcement Letters to Staff

Example for a Returning Principal: This letter can be mailed to staff two weeks before they return to work. It should be welcoming and nonthreatening. Sending a detailed letter about all the changes you want to see will not make for a harmonious opening week with staff. The letter below is from a principal who has been leading a school for one or more years.

Dear Staff,

It is hard to believe the summer has gone by so quickly, and I have enjoyed the slower pace of summer, which allows me time to meet with you, read professional materials, and work with summer school students. This summer, I have enjoyed learning more about our community as well as meeting new staff and the parents of new students. As I write this letter, I feel the surge of excitement I always feel when we start a new school year together.

Please review the enclosed outline of our work week schedule. The schedule allows you as much classroom time as possible. We begin our work week at 8:30 a.m. in the auditorium. A light breakfast will be provided.

I encourage you to enjoy the remainder of your break. Should you have any additional questions, please feel free to give me a call. I look forward to seeing you on August 3.

Sincerely,
Evan Robb

Example for a New Principal: Here is a letter I sent to the staff of the school where I am currently principal. When it was sent, I had been in my new position for approximately six weeks.

Dear Staff:

I hope that you have been enjoying your summer break and involving yourselves in pleasurable and relaxing activities. Soon we will all be back in school beginning what I am sure will be an excellent school year. Many of you have visited me already, and I appreciate how welcoming you have been. Often, when new leadership comes to a school, it can be a time of anxiety and nervousness. This goes both ways. I can assure you that I will do my best to make the transition a smooth and upbeat one for all of us.

Johnson Williams begins the school year with some of the highest test scores in the region. I realize that there are many indicators for success, but in our environment, solid testing is clearly a strong indicator of a successful program. This is quite an accomplishment; it speaks directly to the hard work you do on a daily basis. I want to be one of the first to say, "Great job!" I am excited about being a staff member in such a high-performing school.

I am personally committed to continuous improvement, the belief that all systems in a school can be improved no matter how good they are. Inclusivity in the process is key; I look forward to working with all of you as we work together to make an already excellent school even better! There are only two types of schools in America, those that are improving and those that are declining. There is no middle ground. Given that choice, our path is an obvious one: to improve our school together. Improvement is a never-ending journey. Focusing on getting better assures that each year we move even closer to that goal.

The opening week schedule for staff is included in this mailing. The schedule keeps opening week meetings to a minimum and allows you a great deal of classroom time to prepare for students. I look forward to seeing all of you on our first day back from summer break!

Sincerely,
Evan Robb

I. First-Day Plan

The effective principal cannot be too detailed when explaining how the first day of school will flow. The example below is a plan that I have used with success. This plan is reviewed at the last faculty meeting of the work week before school starts. The effective principal will develop a first-day plan with the assistance of other administrators or staff members. The focus should be on anticipating issues that will develop and working as a team to find answers. No matter how detailed the effective principal thinks the plan is, when he presents it at the faculty meeting, a staff member will attempt to point out a problem. Tell staff any issues they see can be addressed after the meeting. The effective principal avoids going back and forth with staff members in front of the entire faculty. The plan below can be for a new or established middle school or high school. Adjust it to meet the needs of your school.

The First Day of School

- Teachers should arrive before 8:00 a.m. and open their classrooms.
- A teacher from Team XX will greet students who enter the building from the parking lot.
- A teacher from Team XX will greet students who get off buses.
- Team XX will have a teacher in the cafeteria to supervise breakfast.
- Teams XX and XX will have three designated teachers who will monitor the halls before school.
- Many students will want to wander about a new school when they arrive. Some will find their homerooms and enter. Others will be in the halls talking to friends. At 8:21 a.m., a tone will sound. We will announce that students should report to their homerooms. Teachers should be stationed outside their classrooms to greet students as they enter.
- The tone at 8:25 a.m. will mark the beginning of homeroom. Teachers should check and record attendance. Administrative announcements will begin at approximately 8:30 a.m. (This may change if we have several late buses.) The announcements will include the Pledge of Allegiance, any necessary announcements, and a moment of silence.

- Homeroom will last until 9:00 a.m. on Monday. You will need this time to check attendance; hand out homeroom information, which will be in your mailbox on Monday morning; pass out student planners; and inform students about lunch schedules.

If any time remains before we move to first period, you can use it to review usage of the student planner. Discussion of the student planner and county discipline policy can be continued during the study hall after lunch. Please do not distribute lockers during homeroom or study hall on Monday. Students will be overwhelmed, so lockers will be a Day Two activity.

- At 9:00 a.m., a tone will sound. Set a standard on Day One that students leave the room when you dismiss them; they should not get up and leave automatically when the tone sounds. When you dismiss students, they are to report to first period.
- Teachers should be at the door of their room to greet students. Students should arrive before the tardy bell at 9:04 a.m. We will not be marking students tardy for the first week of school. Many students need to learn their way around the school, and we need to assist them. Assist students who can't find their classrooms; they will eventually figure it out with your help. Reinforce to students that we have four minutes between classes. Emphasize that they need to get to class on time. Socializing with a friend is fine, but not when it makes them late to class.
- Please review the following in all classes:
    - The importance of getting to class on time
    - No running in the hallways
    - School procedures for bathroom breaks
- Do not spend your first day with students focusing on rules or punishments. Spend time discussing your class and connecting with kids.
- At 11:49 a.m., XX-grade students who have the first lunch shift will report to the cafeteria. Refer to your list to see which classes report to the cafeteria and which stay in homeroom for study hall. Use this time to continue with whatever needs to be finished from homeroom in the morning. Please wait for an announcement before we switch lunch groups.

- Grade XX will follow the same schedule during their lunch shift, which begins at 12:43 p.m. Again, please wait for an announcement before switching from home room to lunch.

- At 3:05 p.m., the office will make afternoon announcements. Please set the behavioral expectation that students need to be quiet and pay attention to announcements today and every day. Much of the information on Day One will deal with bus departures. Staff has a list of buses and drop-off points; make sure your students know which bus they ride. If students don't know, send them to a designated area so a staff member can help them.

- At 3:07 p.m., the tone will sound. Please dismiss first-wave bus riders, walkers, and students being picked up by car. Other students need to remain in the classroom with you.

- Team XX will send a representative to cover the walkers exiting from the building.

- A health/PE teacher will be on hall duty at this time.

- At 3:20 p.m., all students will be called to the cafeteria area. Music and art teachers will be supervising that area.

- At 4:00 p.m., we will have a brief faculty meeting to review this plan and make any adjustments for Day Two.

J. Math Department Goals for Grades 6, 7, 8

TOPIC	Goals	Action Plan
STUDENT PERFORMANCE	1. All Algebra and Geometry students will take the End-of-Course SOL test on a computer. 2. Any student who fails the Algebra or Geometry SOL test with a 375 or above will receive remediation and will take the test again this school year. 3. All math students will be offered the opportunity to be tutored when necessary. 4a. 100% of our students will pass the Algebra or Geometry SOL Test with 40% passing with an advanced score. 4b. On the Math SOL tests, at least 80% of our students will pass the Math 6 and the Math 7 tests, and at least 89% of our students will pass the Math 8 SOL test. 5. Students with I.E.P.'s will be monitored for SOL readiness.	1a. Algebra and Geometry students will practice taking "SOL type" tests on computers. They will go to the computer lab at least once per month beginning in January. The Jefferson Lab Web site will be used. 1b. Computers will be used during at least 3 classes in May just prior to the SOL test. 2a. Students will receive at least 3 blocks of remediation with teachers before taking the test again. 2b. The test will be given before the end of the school year. 3a. Teachers will offer lunch-time tutoring. 6th- and 7th-grade teachers will offer morning tutoring. The 7th-grade teacher will tutor after school by appointment and on occasion during lunch. 3b. Teachers will post the days and times that they offer tutoring somewhere in their rooms. 3c. Tutoring will begin by the third week of school and will continue throughout the year. 4. Nine-week assessment data will be used to develop daily "Bell Ringers" within 2 weeks of the assessment. 5. Teachers with students with I.E.P.'s will consult at least twice a month with the students' case manager(s).
COMMUNICATION	1. The Math Department will meet at least once a month. 2. All Algebra 1A teachers will meet at least every 2 weeks.	1. Dates of scheduled meetings will be emailed to teachers by the first week of September. 2a. Teachers will meet informally in the hall and formally when arranged by the Department Chair. Minutes will be kept for the formal meetings. 2b. The specific purpose for these meetings will be to keep the Algebra 1A curriculum aligned. 2c. These meetings will begin in September and continue throughout the year.
RECOGNIZING SUCCESS	1. A math student-of-the-week will be selected each full week of the school year. 2. Exceptional math students will be recognized at the end-of-year assembly.	1a. A student-of-the-week will be selected by math teachers. 1b. Teachers will be given dates they will be responsible for at the beginning of the school year. The dates will begin on September 12. 1c. Teachers will fill out an announcement form to be read one day during their week. The student will be given a certificate in their math class that week. 2a. Students who have exhibited excellence during the year in math will be recognized with a "math" t-shirt at the end of the school year. 2b. Criteria for the excellence award will be determined by all teachers in the math department and will be consistent throughout the department.
CONSISTENCY	1. Nine-week cumulative assessments will be the same in each math curricula. 2. All J-WMS students will become familiar with the types of problems on the S.A.T. Test.	1a. Tests will be developed by teachers. 1b. SOL objectives that will be included will be agreed upon for each 9 weeks. 1c. The department will decide how much the test will count toward the student's grade. 2a. Each week, all math teachers will review the SAT problem of the week. 2b. The problems will be written by the Department Chair and will be in the same format as actual S.A.T. questions.

K. Goal-Setting Tips From the Principal

It's natural for teachers to put aside some of the goals they set at the start of school because of the demands of their daily work responsibilities. It's helpful if you can let teachers know that this is okay and periodically redirect their energies back into their goals. Doing this relieves anxieties and stress by sending the message that this is a normal part of goal setting. Here are some things I do at faculty meetings after the winter break to demonstrate that even I have not attended to some goals. Doing this at the halfway mark gives you and teachers time to reevaluate and prioritize goals.

- Share some of the goals I set for myself as an administrator at the start of the school year.
- Point out the goals that I have been able to monitor and those that I have not addressed.
- Explain how you plan to focus your energies on some key goals that have not yet been addressed. Avoid choosing more than two to keep your review of these dropped goals realistic.
- Encourage teachers to independently read and reflect on their goals and place a check next to those they are actively working on or have worked on during the first part of the year.
- Ask teachers to check goals they have met.
- Have teachers study goals that have not been addressed and choose one or two to work on during the second half of the year.
- Assure teachers that you will periodically remind them, through e-mails, to revisit these goals. Tell them you will do the same.

L. Classroom Walk-Through Feedback Forms

Johnson-William M.S.
Classroom Walk-Thru Feedback

Teacher: _____
Subject: _____
Date: _____
Time: _____

Objective: _____

Teaching Behavior: [Teacher . . .]
- Posts class expectations
- Begins class with a warm-up
- Has effective transitions
- Effectively brings class to closure

❑ Concept Presentation
   ❑ Moves around classroom
   ❑ Evidence of student note taking, recording, organization

❑ Questioning
   ❑ Directs questions to individuals
   ❑ Ask questions of many students
   ❑ Allows for adequate response time
❑ Checks for general comprehension by asking for summary, explanation, or evidence
❑ Models appropriate responses
❑ Works with individuals/groups (guided practice)
❑ Monitors independent practice
- Focus on Student Thinking
- Comprehension
   ❑ Analysis
   ❑ Evaluation
   ❑ Application
   ❑ Creativity
- Uses humor
- Connects with students
❑ Is respectful
❑ Other: _____

Teacher Feedback: [Teacher . . .]
❑ Uses positive reinforcement
❑ Provides helpful prompts
❑ Holds students accountable
❑ Makes corrections with dignity

Students Behavior: [Students . . .]
❑ Take notes, record, maintain organization
❑ Ask content questions
❑ Ask probing questions
❑ Work independently
❑ Work in groups
❑ Remain on-task
❑ Remain engaged
❑ Are positively responsive to teacher
❑ Are positively responsive to peers
❑ Demonstrate respect
❑ Demonstrate a sense of community
❑ Are excited, animated
❑ Other: _____

Science Classroom:
❑ Lab procedures are clear
❑ Demonstrates hands-on learning
❑ Models inquiry learning
❑ Students are accountable for labs

Comments:
_____
_____
_____
_____

_____
Observer

(based on a form created by Dr. Mathew Eberhardt,
Assistant Superintendent, Clarke County Schools)

JOHNSON-WILLIAMS M.S.
CLASSROOM WALK-THRU FEEDBACK

Teacher: _Mrs. Johnson_
Subject: _7th Science_
Date: _9-14-06_
Time: _11:00 - 11:20_

Objective: _Apply scientific method to how plants grow_

TEACHING BEHAVIOR: [Teacher...]
- ☑ Posts class expectations
- ☑ Begins class with a warm-up
- ☑ Has effective transitions
- ☑ Effectively brings class to closure
- ☐ CONCEPT PRESENTATION
  - ☐ Moves around classroom
  - ☑ Evidence of student note taking, recording, organization
- ☐ QUESTIONING
  - ☑ Directs questions to individuals
  - ☑ Asks questions of many students
  - ☑ Allows for adequate response time
- ☑ Checks for general comprehension by asking for summary, explanation or evidence
- ☑ Models appropriate responses
- ☑ Works with individuals/groups (guided practice)
- ☑ Monitors independent practice
  - ☐ FOCUS ON STUDENT THINKING
  - ☑ Comprehension
  - ☑ Analysis
  - ☑ Evaluation
  - ☑ Application
  - ☑ Creativity
  - ☑ Uses humor
  - ☑ Connects with students
- ☑ Is respectful
- ☐ Other _____

Good

TEACHER FEEDBACK: [Teacher ...]
- ☑ Uses positive reinforcement
- ☑ Provides helpful prompts
- ☑ Holds students accountable
- ☑ Makes corrections with dignity

Lab activity form

STUDENT BEHAVIOR: [Students...]
- ☑ Take notes, record, maintain organization
- ☑ Ask content questions
- ☑ Ask probing questions
- ☐ Work independently
- ☑ Work in groups
- ☑ Remain on-task
- ☑ Remain engaged
- ☑ Are positively responsive to teacher
- ☑ Are positively responsive to peers
- ☑ Demonstrate respect
- ☑ Demonstrate a sense of community
- ☑ Are excited, animated
- ☐ Other _Very effective lab - excellent class engagement!_

SCIENCE CLASSROOM:
- ☑ Lab procedures are clear — _Posted on chart_
- ☑ Demonstrates hands on learning
- ☑ Models inquiry learning
- ☑ Students are accountable for labs

Comments:
* Consider moving class expectations poster to the front wall
* Circulate the entire classroom

_____
OBSERVER

Based on a form created by Dr. Mathew Eberhardt
Assistant Superintendent, Clarke Co. Schools

M. Monthly Data Summary

Each month as part of a summary of our school initiatives, I send a review to my superintendent. I include an executive summary that gives an overview of the month, along with key data indicators. Superintendents are busy. This document allows my superintendent to read about the school at a time that best suits her needs. My role is to write the summary and compile the data, which comes from various staff members. I do not suggest that the principal be the sole person gathering the data. The data should come to the principal on a specific date each month.

To Dr. Smalley, Superintendent: September Reports on Data and School Initiatives. September has been a busy month. The following is an overview on new initiatives and data:

Mentoring Program: We have developed a new mentor program. The program description expresses the philosophy of mentoring, goals and objectives, assignment of mentors, and a detailed schedule of meetings.

Counselor Watch: This program, which is also documented, formalizes procedures for teams to refer students to guidance. Teams list interventions and select recommended options from a menu of provided services.

Good Friend Program: This program allows teachers to select a small group of students that they keep up with on an informal basis. The program allows teachers to target students who are in different grade levels or not in their classes.

Teacher Evaluation: I have implemented a two-tier approach. Level one is for first-year teachers. The form I created is concrete and covers the fundamentals of solid teaching. Teachers have seen the form and understand the expectations. Evaluation will consist of a pre-evaluation meeting, an evaluation, and a post-evaluation meeting. First-year teachers will receive three formal evaluations during the year. In the second level, teachers from year two and up will use a self-assessment instrument that encourages them to reflect on the four domains of teaching. They evaluate themselves, create meaningful goals, and chart their personal progress throughout the year. In May, I will meet with them to reflect on their goals and to discuss the next level for them. Teachers will provide a summary of their goals and include what progress they made for achieving them.

Student Improvement Plans: I have provided each team with several examples of plans from surrounding counties. They are to look at them as a team and develop a plan that may include components from the other schools. Team leaders will bring their examples back to our school-level team leader meeting, and we will work as a group to develop a plan that includes components of each team's plan. Our completion date should be mid-November. Teams will also develop criteria for placing a student on an improvement plan.

Staff Recognition Program: Our program is titled "First Class Cards." We have a board in the office that staff can use to recognize those who helped make their day easier. Our goal for September was 30 recognitions; we have ended the month with 51! I will track this data monthly.

Blue Jean Friday: Each Friday, staff may wear blue jeans for $1. This money is used to supply staff with food and/or payday treats. Participation has been more than 70 percent for the month of September.

Parent Advisory Committee: This group is now official and meets as an executive board the first Wednesday of each month at 5:00 p.m. Next month, we will form subcommittees to encourage more parental participation.

Back to School Night: This went well. As I noted to you, we had almost 300 parents in attendance.

English Department Initiatives: I have worked with the English Department to develop an aggressive plan for testing improvement. This plan includes a new commitment to the Six Traits writing plan and monthly objectives created by staff to assure alignment is correct. Monthly plans will be turned in to our department chair and copied to me. The department is doing a book study on Six Traits and will report on it October 11. Also, we have designated test preparation books for each grade level. A plan will be developed by the first week of October outlining weekly test preparation objectives for staff. Staff will meet to decide on what sequence they wish to follow per grade level. The Science and Math Departments have been given access to the Jefferson Lab test prep program. This is an online SOL review program that students can use at home or at school.

Yourhomework.com: We have been pushing hard to have staff keep parents up to date on homework assignments as part of our customer service goals. This Web site keeps track of all assignments that teachers give during the year. Currently we have 35 of 46 teachers using yourhomework.com.

In School Plans: These will be finalized by October 11 and be ready to present at the October 13 meeting. Each department in the school has developed a plan focusing on three areas of improvement. The goal is to have all departments, core and non-core subjects, set and focus on goals for the year.

Staff E-mails/Effective School League: Each Monday, staff receives a staff e-mail from me updating them on what is going on for the week, important reminders, and information on school improvement.

Special Education: These teachers have developed specific plans for student performance. You have a copy of those plans.

Our First Curriculum Council Meeting: I've scheduled this for October 5. This will be a monthly meeting of all department chairs. This group will assist in steering our school's instructional program.

Nine-Week Assessments: We are still at the discussion phase. A plan will be finalized on October 5 at the Curriculum Council. These tests will be analyzed according to particular state standards and performance of students who are in AYP subgroup categories.

Additional Data:

- One fire drill per week was conducted for the first four weeks of school. They went very well. Average time to clear the school was two minutes.

- A lockdown drill was completed on September 17.

- A high-wind drill was completed on September 24.

- 59 students were referred to guidance.

- 40 parent contacts were made to guidance.

- 12 interagency consultations took place.

- 24 community service classroom lessons were given.

- The monthly community service parent advisory group met for September.

- 42 new students were given tours.

- Guidance had a pizza lunch with all new students in each grade level.

- In-school suspensions: 38 total; 31 boys, 7 girls; Grade 6: 6; Grade 7: 11; Grade 8: 21

- Suspensions to site: Grade 8: 3

- Assemblies: 1 on September 30

- Library Statistics: 509 items checked out of the library

- Student Attendance: August, 98.13%; September, 94.48%

- Staff Attendance: August, 100%; September. 98.38%

- Home Visits: 8 in September

- Positive Parent Contacts: August, 29; September, 23

N. 15 Top-Notch Books and Articles for Teachers to Investigate

Invite teachers to select books from this list to discuss in study groups. These books also make ideal additions to your school's professional library.

Bamford, M., & Kristo, R. (Eds.) (1998). *Making facts come alive: Choosing quality nonfiction literature K-12*. Norwood, MA: Christopher-Gordon.

Beck, I. L.. & McKeown, M. G. (2006). *Improving comprehension with questioning the author*. New York: Scholastic.

Burke, J. (2000). *Reading reminders: Tools, tips, and techniques*. Portsmouth, NH: Heinemann.

Culham, R. (2003). *6 + 1 traits of writing: The complete guide, grades 3 and up*. New York: Scholastic.

Gallagher, K. (2004). *Deeper reading: Comprehending challenging texts, 4–12*. Portland, ME: Stenhouse.

Gee, J. P. (2000). Teenagers in new times: A new literacy studies perspective. *Journal of Adolescent & Adult Literacy, 43*, 412–420.

Harvey, S., & Goudvis, A. (2000). *Strategies that work: Teaching comprehension to enhance understanding*. York, ME: Stenhouse.

Opitz, M. E. (1998). *Flexible grouping in reading*. New York: Scholastic.

Robb, L. (2000). *Teaching reading in middle school: A strategic approach to reading that improves comprehension and thinking*. New York: Scholastic.

Robb, L. (2003). *Teaching reading in social studies, science, and math: Practical ways to weave comprehension strategies into your content area teaching*. New York: Scholastic.

Robb, L. (2004). *Nonfiction writing from the inside out: Writing lessons inspired by conversations with leading authors*. New York: Scholastic.

Tomlinson, C. A. (1999). *The differentiated classroom: Responding to the needs of all learners*. Alexandria, VA: Association for Supervision and Curriculum Development.

O. Newsletter

THE ROAR

Johnson-Williams Middle School
200 Swan Ave. Berryville, VA 22611
Phone: 540-955-6160 Fax: 540-955-6169
http://jwms.clarke.k12.va.us

MID WINTER 2006

Volume 9 Issue 4

A word from the principal-

January and February may be dreary months but school remains vibrant and full of student enthusiasm. Our student body continues to excel not only academically and in extra curricular activities, but also through service to our community. This month we are collecting canned goods for the Lord Fairfax Community Bank. It makes me proud to see our students' willingness to give back. Also, we had Theatre IV from Richmond perform a show called "Songs from the Soul". I received excellent feedback from students and hope to get this performing group back again next year!

SOL testing is around the corner and I feel confident that our collective efforts will pay off this spring. Departments have been focused on effectively utilizing our 9 week assessments and making classrooms an exciting place to learn.

I am excited about the great possibilities and opportunities here at J-WMS. Student success is a combined effort with the commitment of school, home, and community. Please feel free to visit our school regularly and contact our staff with questions or comments. Customer service is a priority; you and your children are our most important customers and we want to meet your expectations every day.

Sincerely,

Evan Robb, Principal

Additional items:

- Homework is posted at www.yourhomework.com. Parents are encouraged to use this site to access homework!

- The J-WMS Web Site has up to date information on the scroll under the heading "Daily Announcements".

- We will be making a slight change to our afternoon bell schedule, moving to two bells instead of three. This will not impact students getting on buses or car riders.

- Please assist us by using only designated areas for dropping off and picking up your child. Student safety is paramount to us; using designated areas will keep children safe.

- If your schedule allows, we would appreciate your presence at athletic events.

Dates to Remember:

January:
30-Feb. 3 - SCA Spirit Week

February:
1- Academic Awards: 8th grade, 8:30 a.m.
        7th grade, 9:15 a.m.
        6th grade, 10:05 a.m.
3 - J-WMS Spelling Bee, 8:45 a.m.
  - SCA Winter Social, 1:30 - 3:00 p.m.
22 - County Wide Spelling Bee, 9:00 a.m.
27 - March 1 - Volleyball Tryouts, 7th grade 3:30-5
        8th grade 5-6:30

Looking Ahead:
March 17, 18 and 19 - the musical "Fiddler on the Roof" performances will be held in the Williams Community Auditorium at J-WMS. Friday and Saturday shows are at 7:30 p.m. Sunday's show begins at 2 p.m.

Tickets are sold at the door only!

The 8th Grade Update

The 8th grade has already begun gearing up for their SOL tests. The teachers are working on test-taking strategies. We will kick off the SOL testing week with an 8th grade pep-rally/talk on March 2. To celebrate their success at J-WMS, the 8th grade will be going to Hershey Park on June 2ndl Information will be sent home in February with details, permission forms and field trip costs.

Page 2

THE ROAR

February 2006

Virginia
School
Board
Appreciation
Month

More Than A Million Thanks!

☆☆

Fiddler on the Roof is up and running!

"Tradition!" A word at the heart of the annual spring musical program, is the very essence of the beloved "Fiddler on the Roof." This sixth installment features 50 CCPS students (grades 6-12) in the cast, and a pit band of 20 made up mostly of middle school students.

All of the favorite songs and scenes, and a good deal of Jerome Robbins' original choreography will be presented in front of a fantastic set. Mark your calendars: shows are Friday and Saturday, March 17 and 18 at 7:30 p.m. and Sunday, March 19 at 2 p.m. Tickets are $10 for adults and $5 for students, **sold only at the door.** Come and be entertained and amazed by the talent of our scholar performers!

L'Chaim!

☆☆

Second Nine Weeks Honor Roll

6th Grade Alpha: Daniel Bailey, Heidi Crockett, Charles Cunningham, Caitlin Fikac, Amanda Gordon, Levi Hagerdon, Kristen Hopkins, Jessica Isleib, Colin Johnson, Brogan Jones, Conor Mettenburg, Courtney Rogers, Connor Shendow, and Megan Waring.

6th Grade Beta: Christopher Andrae, Cody Ash, Brittany Baraquio, James Barber, Katelyn Barnhill, Eva Blau, Allen Bridge, Courtney Butterfass, Sabrina Callan, Julianna Cantrell, Tabatha Chandler, Brandon Christian, James Cochran, Kaylyn Colvin, Thomas Combs, Lauren Daniels, Noah Dashner, Paul Davis, Zachary DeMoss, Nelson Drake, Michaela Garrison, Jesse Givens, Christina Hash, Rachel Hickey, Julia Johnston, Daniel Judge, Jamie Lamphier, Denya Dee Leake, Chelsea Lepley, Peter Levi, Kathleen Longerbeam, Benjamin Marshall, Timothy May, Brendan McGrath, Simon McKay, Matthew Miller, Maris Mulroney, Jessica Myer, Sophia Neuber, Chase Ohm, Brandon Payne, Samantha Pearson, Richard Ramey, Kristine Raymond, Jesse Robinson, Samantha Saylor, Alexander Sefton, Jesse Smoot, Elliot Symonds, Taylor Thompson, Donald Tredway, Rachel Vinson, Monica Warfield, Jacob Webb, Sidney Wilkins, Nicole Willingham, Mikaela Wilson, Natalie Wright, and Steven Zumbaugh.

7th Grade Alpha: Katherine Ashby, Daniel Barley, Caleb Biggs, Rachel Boag, Michelle Brown, Kasey Canterbury, Emma Cohen, Lindsay Dennis, Brianna Harrell, Dixie Hurtado, Logan Johnson, Rebecca Jones, James Kerby, Emily Lantz, Valory Lohmann, Katlyn Mercke, Matthew Moyer, Alana Murphy, Victoriana Pitre, Brendan Rogers, Katherine Steinmetz, and Kayla Ward.

7th Grade Beta: Chase Anderson, Jessica Anderson, Kristina Beecroft, Stephan Bodkin, Matthew Callis, Jackie Carter, Thomas Cleary, Anastasia Donner, Michael Flagg, Caitlin Friess, Jasmine Grant, Catherine Hall, Ashley Jenkins, Brittany Keesling, Alexandra Kuehm, Colleen Lentile, Chelsea Levi, Anna Louthan, Rebecca Mason, Riley McCall, Jordan McClung, Ellie Meyer, Aiza Montini, Zachary Myer, Stephanie Nicholson, Megan Noble, Katlyn O'Donnell, Katherine Orndorff, Caitlin Petrosky, Blake Place, Benjamin Poe, Zachary Rhoads, Meredith Roberts, Elizabeth Stewart, Alexis Stickovitch, Clara Thiel, Steven Trayer, Kevin Wadley, William Wallace, Taylor Wann, Reid Welliver, Megan Wilson, Cody Wisecarver, and Rebecca York.

8th Grade Alpha: Daniel Amundson, Nicholas Andrae, Stefani Bell, Daniel Borger, Adam Campbell, Kaitlyn Dykes, Sarah Elliston, Kathryn Lettie, Jodi Noland, Katherine Roberts, Karoline Seekford, Regan Sheets, Rylee Shull, Meghan Snapp, Devin Stiles, Thomas Trapnell, Frederick Twigg, Nathan Veilleux, and Kevin Wiseman.

8th Grade Beta: Christina Applewood, Leslie Asan, Devon Barr, Jade Barr, Kristen Bergner, Elijah Biddle-Snead, Kevin Broderick, Colin Brown, Joshua Case, Samuel Creany, Amber Desjardins, Ilia Donner, Janet George, Christa Goad, Jacob Griffith, Amy Hagerdon, Thomas Hickey, Carol Jackson, Molly Keesling, Caitlin Leach, Britney Leaf, Kathryn Lese, Morgan Lockhart, Robert Madden, Isabelle Masters, Amanda Nubih, Kevin Nina, Adam Owens, Jenna Parke, William Purker, Russell Reid, Airiel Renner, Alexander Santese, Jordan Shepherd, Amy Short, Holly Smucker, Mauriciao Tellez-Nava, Mason Thompson, Tyler Thompson, Meredith Vaughn, Zachary Webb, and Samantha Wiltrout.

Congratulations on your achievement!

Amazing amounts of information are at the

CCPS Website

Visit it today at http://www.clarke.k12.va.us/

- SOL Practice
- School Menus and Calendars
- Up-to-the-minute School Closing and Delay Information
- Special Summer Programs
- Employment Opportunities

To contribute to our web site, contact PJ Dempsey:

dempseyp@clarke.k12.va.us

PTO NEWS

The J-WMS PTO is signing up for Box Tops 4 Education to earn extra cash for the school. Each "Box Top" is worth 10 cents, so the more cut out and collected, the higher the return.

To participate, please bring your cut out box tops to the office in an envelope or baggie to place in the container which will be a General Mills cereal box. The deadline for the 2005-06 school year is Tuesday, February 28.

"Do I send my child to school??"

Just a reminder…DO NOT send your child to school if ANY of these symptoms or signs are present in the previous 24 hours:

Vomiting, nausea, and abdominal pain, elevated temperature (100 degrees or higher), repeated diarrhea, acute cold, sore throat or persistent cough, unusual or lethargic behavior.

There will be times when it is difficult to tell when your child is too ill to go to school. Like adults, children have very different tolerances to discomfort or illness.

If you decide to send your child to school when he/she is on the "borderline" of being ill, it is a good idea to call the school to let us know where you can be contacted in case your child's condition worsens.

Clarke County Public Schools/J-WMS
309 West Main Street
Berryville, VA 22611

U.S. POSTAGE
NON-PROFIT ORG.
PAID
PERMIT NO. 3088
